The
Damp House

Jonathan Hetreed

THE CROWOOD PRESS

First published in 2008 by
The Crowood Press Ltd
Ramsbury, Marlborough
Wiltshire SN8 2HR

www.crowood.com

This impression 2014

British Library Cataloguing-in-Publication Data
A catalogue record for this book is available from the British Library.

ISBN 978 1 86126 966 9

Disclaimer
The author and publisher do not accept responsibility or liability in any manner
whatsoever for any omission, nor any loss, damage, injury, or adverse outcome of
any kind incurred as a result of the use of the information contained in this book,
or reliance upon it. Readers are advised to seek professional advice relating to
their particular property and circumstances before beginning any damp treatment
or any form of remedial building work.

Photo Credits
Front and back cover photographs and Figs 81, 100, 101, and 142
by Shelagh Hetreed.
Figs 15, 25, 79, 147 and 148 by Andrew Smith of Peter Cox
Property Services.
Fig. 92 by Martine Hamilton-Knight of MHK Photography.
121 and 125 by Passivent Ltd.
All other photographs are by the author.

Typeset by Exeter Premedia Services Private Ltd., Chennai, India

Printed and bound in Malaysia by Times Offset (M) Sdn Bhd

Contents

Introduction and Acknowledgements

Dampness is the stuff of life: without it our land-world would be dead but, like weeds – often beautiful plants simply growing in the wrong place – dampness becomes an enemy when it invades our interior space, when it persists, spreads and damages the finishes, fittings – and contents – of our homes. In some cases, it can encourage the growth of moulds that threaten our health, as well as stimulating fungus and decay in the structure of a house. It is one of the commonest problems noted by surveyors assessing houses for sale and frequently, its eradication is a condition for buyers obtaining mortgages.

A major industry has developed offering 'damp treatments' to home owners, many of them with guarantees – though these are often short-lived and beset with conditions – but specialist contractors often concentrate on a single treatment rather than offering a comprehensive diagnosis. The aim of this book is to provide clear information to general readers and to present them with an overview of the types and causes of dampness, as well as to indicate the range of treatments and remedies.

Since no two individual circumstances are the same, no book can provide all the answers and there is no substitute for experienced, expert diagnosis and advice. However, clear explanations of the symptoms, causes and mechanisms of dampness, as well as descriptions of the methods used to combat it, should help readers to understand and solve simple problems themselves, as well as to evaluate various solutions offered to them by professionals.

ACKNOWLEDGEMENTS

There are so many to thank for a career in architecture that involves constant learning from one's own and others' experience.

Clive Gaynard of Timsbury Preservation has taught me more about the practicalities of damp treatment over 27 years than anyone else, and always with an honesty and wit that has maintained my faith in the industry – even when others sorely tried it!

My former colleagues at Feilden Clegg and my current colleagues at Hetreed Ross, along with so many contractors and specialists, building control officers and conservationists, have contributed immensely to the experience from which this book has been gleaned.

Published material used in my research appears in the list of Further Reading at the end of the book: the Building Research Establishment has been an invaluable source of theoretical and practical material.

There have been detailed contributions from many others to my research for the book, and to the photographs included. I would particularly like to thank: Wraxall Builders; Bath and NE Somerset Building Control; Aaron Roofing; the Mastic Asphalt Council; Peter Cox Property Services; Timber Decay Treatment; Permagard Products; Cotswold Treatments; Leo Wood, master thatcher; Roofkrete; Gledhill Water Storage; Hepworth Building Products; Passivent; Wessex Water.

Thanks are due to The Crowood Press for sound advice, patience and sympathy. I would also thank Shelagh, Lisa and Kelly for putting up with my too frequent neglect of them while I wrote the book.

DEDICATION

To my father, Dr Bill Hetreed, whose lifelong enthusiasm for both the theories and the messy practicalities of making things had much to do with my becoming an architect and enjoyer of building.

CHAPTER 1

Definitions and Diagnosis

The causes of dampness are often difficult to diagnose, sometimes because the problems are hidden, though the symptoms may be all too visible, and sometimes because there are several causes acting simultaneously. Neglected houses are likely to have suffered from lack of maintenance in many ways; misguided or inexpert attempts to cure dampness often fail and sometimes make matters worse, or, by concealing the symptoms, make diagnosis more difficult. Before discussing diagnosis in more detail, it will be useful to establish some clear definitions.

RISING DAMP

This is the classic form of damp that most people mean when they think of a damp house. As the term implies, it consists of moisture from the ground rising in porous wall construction by means of capillary action, in the same way that oil rises in the wick of an oil lamp, but in buildings the wall is the 'wick' and the moisture in the ground is the 'oil'. Classic visual signs are the 'tide mark' of damp staining or decayed finishes, often reaching to around a metre above local external ground levels.

PENETRATING DAMP

This consists of moisture – usually rain, occasionally floods – penetrating the interior of the house from the outside, under wind or gravity. There are many parts to the 'envelope' or external skin of a house – roofs, walls, windows, doors, chimneys and so on – each of which have their own sets of components (for example, in the tiles, slates, flashings, copings, ridges

of roofs) and each of these components has its own role to play in keeping out the weather. Consequently, damage, deterioration or dislodging of even individual components can lead to damp penetration or a full-scale leak, though such is the complexity of construction, particularly modern or modernized construction with its multiple layers, that the symptoms may not necessarily appear where they are expected.

The visual signs of penetrating damp may well seem similar to those of rising damp but they usually relate more specifically to local sources and will, therefore, vary markedly around the house; for example, a sheltered wall may appear dry, whereas one fully exposed to driving rain from the prevailing westerly

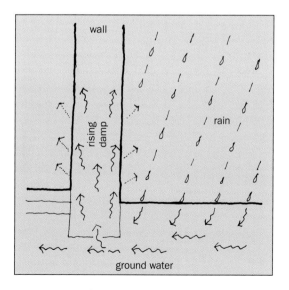

Fig 1   Rising damp – uses walls as wicks.

5

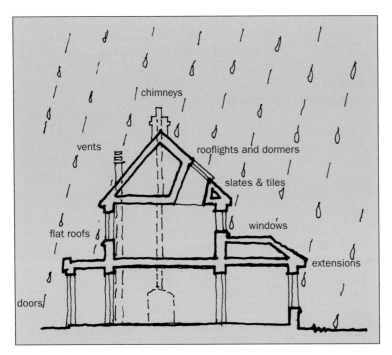

Fig 2   Penetrating damp – every external component is vulnerable.

wind may be seriously affected, or even more specifically, a spreading vertical damp patch that is worst at the top of a wall may relate to a leaking rainwater pipe or broken gutter.

CONSTRUCTION MOISTURE

For most domestic construction in the UK, wet materials and processes are used both for new homes and in alterations, principally in concrete, masonry, plastering, screeding and decorating. For a typical masonry-built semi-detached house, around 8t or 8,000ltr of water are embodied in its construction; although around half of this water will usually have evaporated by the time the house is completed, the drying-out process will continue for at least six months and sometimes much longer if it is delayed by damp weather or if built-in dampness has been exacerbated by poor construction management. The same process happens with extensions, improvements and alterations, though usually to a lesser extent.

Although there are many good reasons to speed up construction and get projects completed as quickly as possible, drying-out is not one of them, at least in

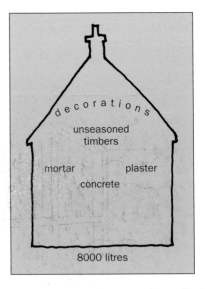

Fig 3   Construction moisture – 8t of water built into a three-bedroom masonry house.

traditional construction. Where sufficient time has not been allowed for drying-out before finishes are applied – a common rule of thumb is that a month of 'good drying conditions' (i.e. dry air and lots of ventilation) should be allowed for every 25 mm (1in) of 'wet construction' such as a concrete slab – symptoms of damp may well appear and can give the impression of serious faults: these should be relatively short-lived but may cause minor damage to decorations, for example, and may need minor treatment if salts are brought to the surface (*see below*). The obvious clues to construction moisture are its association with new (wet) work and its diminishing over time.

CONDENSATION

This is probably the most complicated form of dampness, often difficult to diagnose and sometimes occurring as 'interstitial condensation' between the layers of a buildings structure, where it can remain invisible to the occupants for years, while it contributes to problems such as timber decay.

Put most simply, condensation occurs when warm moisture-laden air (water vapour) meets a cold surface, with the most familiar and conspicuous example probably being the water droplets forming on the inside of a window in a steamy shower room. It occurs most often in winter when houses are least ventilated and when uninsulated external walls, windows, and so on, are at their coldest; but it can also occur in summer, often on interior walls or chimney breasts that are cool in relation to warm, humid external air. It is particularly affected by people's management of their homes; for example, in the extent of ventilation and control of moisture sources such as cooking and washing.

Signs of condensation, less obvious than water droplets on windows, are often grey or black-spotted mould growth on walls and ceilings, particularly to areas with least air movement, such as corners or recesses, and colder areas of construction around windows and doors, or below uninsulated roofs.

LEAKING SERVICES AND APPLIANCES

Major improvements to the convenience and comfort of houses have included bringing water supply and drainage inside the 'building envelope', which naturally brings the attendant risk of failure in these 'services' – usually in the form of leaking pipes or tanks – causing dampness. Leaking external pipes and drains, whether above or below ground, can also cause damp problems by supplying the water that leads to penetrating or rising damp. Leaking water-supply pipes can be particularly troublesome in this respect because the supply of water is continuous, rather than intermittent, as from rain or drainage. Some of the wet appliances we use – principally washing machines and dishwashers – tend to have a much shorter life than our piped services; even relatively minor faults such as failure of seals can lead to damaging internal flooding, particularly if left undetected. Most of our 'sanitary ware' – baths, basins, sinks, showers and lavatories – is reliable and long-lasting but small leaks can go undetected for long periods, especially from shower cubicles and trays, where the advent of the 'power shower' has strained the performance of finishes and seals, and this can lead to cumulative damp problems, often hidden, initially, in floor structures.

SALT CONTAMINATION

As moisture migrates through walls, whether from driving rain or from rising damp or any other cause, it tends to evaporate from inside surfaces to leave

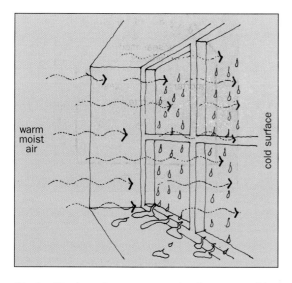

Fig 4   Condensation – warm moist air meets a cold surface.

warm moist air

cold surface

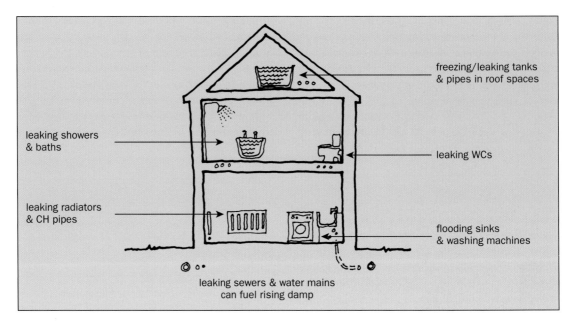

Fig 5   Leaking sewers and appliances.

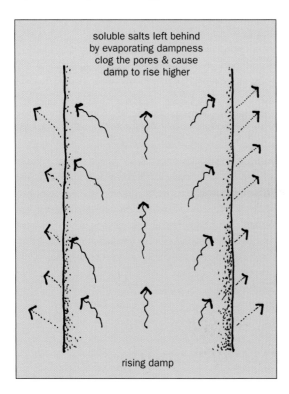

Fig 6   Salt contamination from evaporating moisture.

increasing mineral salt concentration in the inner face of the wall, for example. Some of these salts may appear as fine crystals on the surface of the wall, and some of them may be hygroscopic, meaning that they tend to absorb moisture from the air, which then tends to prolong the effects of dampness after the original source has dried up. This fact and the long periods needed to dry out damp walls after a damp course has been formed, lead to damp-proofing specialists insisting on removal of plaster (often salt contaminated) and its replacement with proprietary salt-inhibiting render mixes as part of their specification.

DAMP-PROOF COURSES (DPCs)

The term is self-explanatory, though a little confusing if you are reading a label on a roll of polythene strip – how can this be a 'course'? When first widely introduced in the late nineteenth century – the Public Health Act of 1875 made them compulsory in new dwellings – damp-proof courses consisted of a course or, preferably, several courses of impervious bricks or of slates, which are more susceptible to cracking so tend to be less reliable than brick courses.

Single courses of any material are weakest at the joints, since mortars are seldom reliably waterproof, particularly the weaker, more flexible mortars that are least likely to crack. Cracks in mortar joints are a further cause of failure in rigid damp courses.

Flexible damp-course materials have followed the development of the chemical industry in their changing materials and increasing toughness and flexibility; relatively costly metal DPCs, particularly lead and occasionally copper, were used in high-specification buildings, while cheaper flexible DPCs were made from hessian-reinforced bitumen, until the adoption of plastics from the 1950s onwards rendered them increasingly obsolete. Hybrid 'pitch-polymer' materials were popular in the 1970s and 80s but have been criticized for health reasons, leaving the market dominated by 'pure plastics' from plain black polythene to more sophisticated polymers.

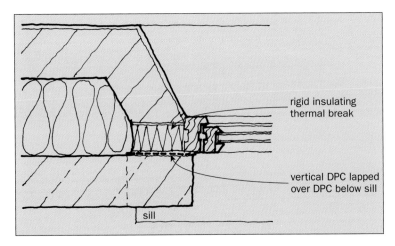

Fig 7 Detail plan of vertical DPC at a window in a cavity wall.

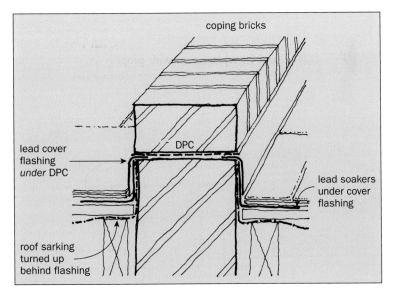

Fig 8 Detail of DPC to copings above roofs.

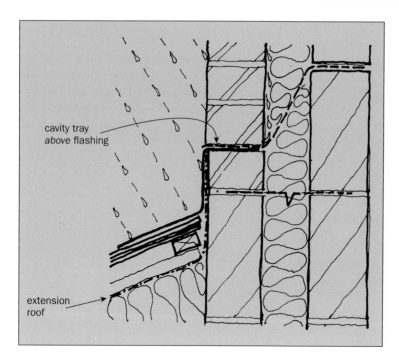

Fig 9 DPC cavity tray at roof abutment.

cavity tray *above* flashing

extension roof

Although flexible DPCs have major advantages of relative freedom from joints, flexibility to withstand movement in masonry, ease of use and low cost, they do have limitations, particularly in adhesion to themselves for sealing joints at corners, roll-ends and stepped details (where the need for specific adhesives and clean conditions make site management and workmanship critical), and to mortar where their very flexibility causes them to form a slip plane, which effectively 'detaches' a wall from its foundation.

In substantial buildings, stability is maintained by the sheer weight of masonry, but free-standing walls, particularly smaller garden walls, can be vulnerable to high winds or modest impacts due to flexible DPCs, so are still often built with brick, tile or slate DPCs at the base and the coping, or else have DPCs omitted entirely.

DPCs are fitted in modern construction – and in alterations – to protect against penetrating damp, as well as rising damp, particularly around openings in cavity walls where the window or door 'reveals' close the cavity and would otherwise provide a route for moisture to enter the house. DPCs at coping level, where walls project above roofs, for example. are especially important in preventing the downward entry of moisture. Another critical point, equally applicable in alterations and extensions, is where roofs adjoin higher external walls, particularly cavity walls: the DPC in this location is called a cavity tray and will be discussed in more detail in Chapter 3.

Retro-fitted or remedial DPCs are occasionally physical sheet barriers inserted into slots cut through walls but more often proprietary systems of chemical injection, electronic treatment or evaporation devices. These are dealt with fully in Chapter 2.

DAMP-PROOF MEMBRANES (DPMs)

Serving the same purpose as DPCs – preventing rising damp – but across ground floors, DPMs have followed a similar but later evolution. Although the model by-laws of 1937 required damp-proofing – usually of pitch or bitumen – between solid floors and timber finishes, it was not until the 1950s that they were increasingly adopted beneath solid concrete floors, and they were not mandatory under the Building Regulations until 1967. Prior to the reliable and cheap production of polythene sheeting, DPMs were formed either from liquid bitumen or trowelled asphalt, or from waterproof building papers laminated with bitumen. Good quality concrete floor slabs, particularly of at least 150mm (6in) thickness, are generally waterproof and their performance can be improved by additives; but thinner slabs, such as the 100mm (4in) slabs generally used in housing, are less reliable and the addition of a DPM is a simple and effective measure, which has the beneficial side-effect of improving the quality of the concrete by retaining water and fine aggregate ('fines') within the mix.

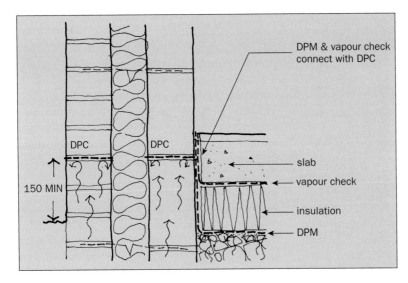

Fig 10   DPCs and DPM for a solid ground floor.

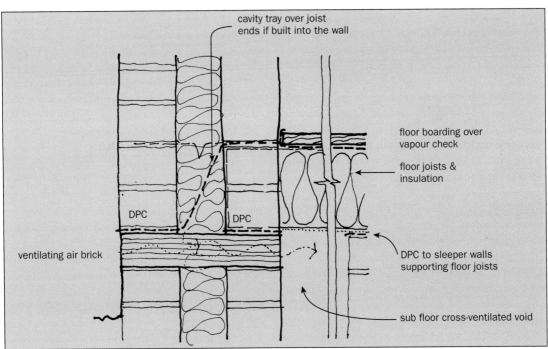

Fig 11   DPCs and ventilation for timber ground floor.

The weak points of DPMs are at their joints and where they join wall DPCs; although most details are straightforward, good workmanship is critical, particularly for floors below adjacent ground levels. Traditional timber, suspended ground floors include no DPMs but rely on cross ventilation to prevent dampness accumulating and causing decay; accidental or sometimes deliberate blocking of such sub-floor vents (to prevent draughts entering the house) is one of the commonest causes of decay and failure of timber ground floors in houses.

Once cheap, flexible DPCs were introduced, they began to be used – though inconsistently – to protect timber joists from rising damp in supporting walls. In older timber floors, slate was sometimes used under joists for the same reason.

VAPOUR CHECKS

The commonest form of vapour check in construction is clear polythene sheet, usually thinner at 125μ (1000-guage) than the 250 or 300μ (500-guage) sheet used for DPMs, and transparent (instead of black or blue) because it is usually needed internally, so is less exposed to sunlight (and its destructive ultraviolet rays), and because seeing through it makes fixing and checking easier. In most construction, 'barrier' is a misnomer since mere fixing perforates it, and the idea of a barrier to vapour can be a dangerous illusion – it is important that construction details outside the vapour check allow for the inevitable leaks of vapour and for its dispersal. Only in special circumstances, with great care on site, can a true vapour barrier be formed, which then has to be protected against future damage; for example, in the insertion of wiring or light fittings.

The role of the vapour check is to hold back water vapour on the inside of construction, so as to reduce the amount reaching cold external materials and condensing. Its importance is in direct proportion to the susceptibility of the construction to damp and to the impermeability of the cold exterior: to take a worst example, an insulated timber-framed roof closely covered in metal sheeting, but without an effective vapour check, may appear to be leaking due to the quantity of condensation dripping back through the ceiling – and probably rotting the timbers. The same construction with a polythene sheet vapour check on the inside of the insulation, and a ventilated cavity under the metal sheet, should be trouble-free.

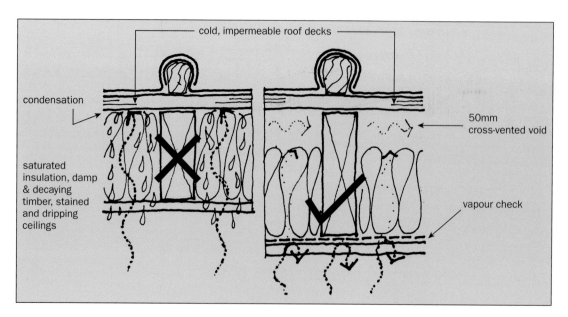

Fig 12   Vapour check and ventilation to minimize condensation below impermeable roofs.

As floors have been increasingly insulated – particularly if the floor is heated – vapour checks have become more widely used, always on the warm side of the insulation, below the flooring and over the joists in timber floors, and over the insulation in concrete floors; in contrast to the DPM, which is usually next to the ground or hardcore.

There has been some negative reaction to the 'sealed-house approach' and, particularly, to vapour checks, which suggests that more natural internal conditions in houses and better air quality are achieved by 'breathing construction', which allows air and vapour to pass slowly through it in either direction. So as to avoid or to minimize condensation, it is then critical that there is a gradient of permeability through the construction from the less permeable inside to the most permeable outside, which allows the condensation occurring in the outer layers of

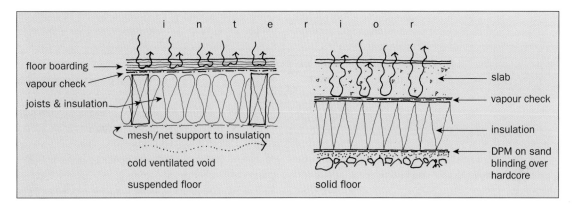

Fig 13 Vapour checks in solid and suspended ground floors.

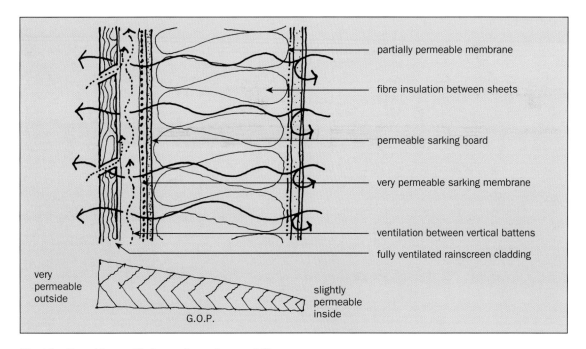

Fig 14 'Breathing wall': the gradient of permeability.

13

insulation to evaporate harmlessly through well-ventilated cladding (over timber or steel framing) or vapour-tolerant construction (usually masonry). Manufacturers have developed special 'vapour-control' sheetings for the inside and 'vapour-permeable' sheetings for the outside.

SYMPTOMS AND DIAGNOSIS

The most blatant symptom of dampness is water itself, common enough from condensation and from leaks, whether from rain or faulty pipework, easy to see and sometimes to hear; it is also relatively easy to trace, though significant dismantling may be needed to track its path. Subtler symptoms, such as damp patches, peeling paint or wallpaper, and a whole range of moulds and fungi, from the slight mottling of incipient grey or black moulds, due to intermittent condensation, to the full glories of the fruiting bodies of 'dry rot' (a confusing name for the fungus *Serpula lacrymans*, that thrives in damp but not wet conditions), can be caused by many different kinds of dampness or by a combination of them. As a result, diagnosis can be much more difficult; a process of elimination may be required over a considerable period to be sure of a correct result. The complexity of diagnosis is further increased by the human factor: different occupants and lifestyles in otherwise similar houses can generate quite different problems or, in some cases, no problems at all; whereas a neighbour may suffer seriously from the symptoms of damp.

Similarly, people's attitudes to damp vary enormously. Historically, buildings were expected to be damp if they were built in damp places, and most people lived a generally weather- and damp-tolerant existence. They relied on ventilation, damp-tolerant materials and careful placing of their possessions to avoid or mitigate the problems of living in damp houses. During the twentieth century, the people of industrial societies have experienced steadily 'rising standards of living' and changing attitudes to public health and housing conditions, which mean that a damp house is now considered somewhat disgraceful, as well as unhealthy and damaging to itself, its finishes and contents, as well as its occupants.

As the costs and awareness of the environmental effects of profligate energy use have grown, we have been encouraged to 'seal up' our houses with draft-stripping and insulation. Both measures tend to increase comfort and reduce energy use but can exacerbate some of the symptoms of damp, particularly if the improvements are partial or piecemeal; for example, in draft-stripping windows that remain single

Fig 15   Fruiting bodies of dry rot fungus. (Peter Cox)

glazed, which will tend to increase condensation since there will be much less ventilation across the glass.

MULTIPLE DIAGNOSIS

Similar symptoms may derive from different causes and, particularly in derelict or poorly maintained houses, there may be several sources of damp-producing symptoms simultaneously. Unlike a human patient discussing their symptoms with their doctor, the damp house is mute and can sometimes represent a serious challenge even to experts. Rapid diagnosis is particularly risky, since both time and climate tend to affect symptoms; as well as a thorough survey, potentially including taking material samples from walls and floors for analysis, it may prove necessary to assess the building over a period of time, including different weather conditions.

It may be clear initially that penetrating damp is a problem – for example, from the holes in the roof – but the extent to which rising damp is also present may not become clear until some time after the roof is repaired and drying-out has begun. Similarly, condensation may not show up as a problem until winter, or until new occupants dramatically increase the amount of hot water and steam in a house, while reducing ventilation rates.

The Building Research Establishment (BRE)'s guidance on damp assessment suggests an 8-point process for thorough diagnosis:

1. Check for recent construction changes in the affected areas (for example, new openings made, ground levels altered, or cavity walls altered or insulated), that may not have been correctly detailed.
2. Record visually, by photographs or sketches, the exact location of penetrating moisture.
3. Record in the same way any staining or mould growth.
4. Record local context, such as neighbouring buildings, trees, and so on, particularly noting any recent changes that may have affected the building's exposure to weather.
5. Record timing of moisture appearing and drying-out, in relation to weather conditions, including

any time-lags between changes in weather and changes in damp symptoms.
6. Measure the moisture content of the affected construction, initially by meter testing and then by sampling and laboratory analysis; take samples from the full thickness of construction rather than just from surfaces.
7. Measure and record the weather externally and conditions internally: temperature, humidity, wind and rain or snow.
8. Open up the affected construction to check exactly how it is built, taking care not to obscure the 'track' of moisture from its source.

Clearly, some of these checks are easier than others and it is seldom necessary to go as far as laboratory analysis of samples to diagnose straightforward problems, even with multiple causes; but too rapid an assessment can easily lead to simplistic solutions and thereby to unnecessary costs. The scale of diagnosis – and of remedies – should also match both the scale of the problem and the level of need: many people live quite happily in slightly damp, traditionally built houses, so the fact that a local damp problem appears, or gets worse, may require an appropriate local solution but does not mean that the whole house suddenly 'needs treatment'.

Conversely, more modern houses typically incorporate damp-resistant details and materials, so damp problems are likely to be due to damage or decay, or to incorrect construction or alteration, which should be relatively simple to remedy, as long as the existing details are thoroughly checked before remedial works are decided. For example, a house that has had its damp course 'bridged' by increased ground levels or new rendering down to the ground, should not need a new damp course; rather, it needs its ground levels or new render amended so that the damp course has a chance to work as it should.

At the other end of the scale, the long-derelict house may be thoroughly saturated and suffering from most forms of dampness and decay: its restoration and improvement will very likely involve most of the symptoms and many of the remedies described in this book, at various stages through its decline and recovery. Although elaborate testing and material sampling may not be needed, it can have advantages

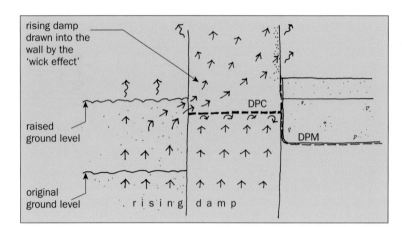

Fig 16   DPC 'bridged' by raised ground levels.

in distinguishing different sources of damp. In the saturated derelict house, it may still be possible to tell at an early stage, before drying-out, whether there is rising damp as well as penetrating damp, for example, by sampling the core material of walls at several levels: if moisture content decreases significantly with height, rising damp will almost certainly be a part of the equation. Once core moisture content is tested at below 5 per cent, rising damp is unlikely to be present.

CHAPTER 2

Rising Damp

HOW IT OCCURS

There are three preconditions for rising damp: ground contact, ground moisture and porous construction.

Ground Contact

By definition, therefore, walls and ground floors are vulnerable. The DPCs and DPMs of modern construction work by breaking that ground contact. At a damp site, such defences have to be thorough and consistent: rising damp is remarkably successful in showing up poor construction.

Ground Moisture

Ground moisture is not so simple, since it varies markedly both in time and place. A single house can show completely different conditions; for example, between a back wall that is built into a hill and a front wall that is built up above lower ground – if the water-table (the level of ground moisture) follows the profile of the hill (often but not always so), then the back wall can be saturated while the front wall is entirely dry. The water-table tends to fall in summer and rise in winter, due to varying rainfall and to evaporation rates and transpiration from trees and plants; this can lead in borderline cases to purely seasonal damp problems, though there may be a gradual worsening of the symptoms due to the build up of mineral salts (*see below*).

Porous Construction

Masonry materials, brick and stone, and to a lesser extent concrete, are the best-known sufferers from rising damp, but any porous construction material, for example, timber, plaster or earth – usually found

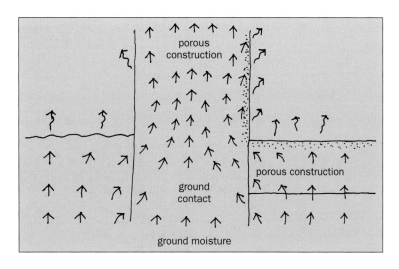

Fig 17   Preconditions for rising damp.

17

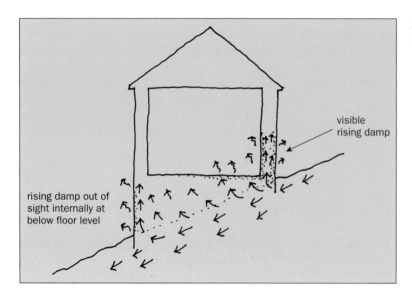

Fig 18   Rising damp can vary within one house.

visible rising damp

rising damp out of sight internally at below floor level

as cob, clay lump or similar in traditional houses and as rammed earth or unfired clay blocks in modern construction – may be a victim in the wrong circumstances.

Conversely, non-porous building materials, steel, glass, very dense bricks (for example, engineering bricks) and a few impervious stones such as slate, do not support rising damp and, in the case of the dense bricks and slates, are used as damp-proof construction materials.

The relevant difference between these two groups of materials is in their pore structure: the damp-prone materials have an open-pore structure, which transmits moisture by capillary action. The extent to which this happens depends on four main factors:

1. The pore structure of the construction material.
2. The degree of saturation of the ground.
3. The rate of evaporation.
4. The concentration of salts in the material's surfaces.

Although rising damp in walls typically reaches to around a metre above adjacent ground levels, local conditions produce wide variations. Generally, the smaller the pore size, the higher the damp rises; pores as small as a thousandth of a millimetre are not uncommon in traditional materials, including bricks. Local variations in the water-table with high ground close to a house,

even though not actually touching it, can cause higher damp levels.

The effect of evaporation is again most pronounced in fine-pored material; evaporation rates increase with temperature – so in summer, and with heating, this in turn stimulates the rising damp, though its effects may be less visible because of the faster evaporation from the surface. Reduced symptoms in summer due to increased evaporation are reinforced by falling water-tables.

As moisture rises from the ground, soluble mineral salts are carried up through the wall or floor, along with further minerals dissolved from the construction materials themselves. As the moisture evaporates from the surface, it leaves the mineral salts behind in gradually increasing concentrations, which crystallize out and gradually block the pores, so encouraging following moisture to rise higher to 'achieve evaporation'(*see* Fig 6).

Some mineral salts are hygroscopic, attracting atmospheric moisture; as these concentrate at surfaces, they collect dampness from the atmosphere, so that in humid conditions, walls and floors can feel clammy to the touch even though rising damp may not be present; for example, in the summer. This effect can easily be confused with condensation appearing in similar weather on cold, internal masonry (*see* Chapter 4).

Although surface accumulation of mineral salts is a classic symptom of rising damp, it can occur as a result of any form of dampness, since it is merely a product of evaporation of moisture – how the moisture gets into the material does not dictate how it gets out. Flooding can temporarily saturate the base of walls and floors – regardless of DPCs and DPMs – and then take months or even years to dry out. Persistent penetrating damp can, by force of gravity, accumulate moisture at the base of a wall and in floors, which in the process of evaporation can behave just like rising damp, bringing the salts to the surface.

WHEN DOES IT OCCUR?

Failure

It is unusual, but possible, for DPCs and DPMs to fail – particularly early, 'flexible' DPCs of hessian-reinforced bitumen can become compressed and embrittled with age, so that they cease to be flexible and the hessian may simply disintegrate. The combination of ageing DPC material and even minor settlement in foundations can be enough to crack DPCs. Movement will also effect rigid damp-proof courses of slate, tile or brick, and may cause cracking of the mortar or of the material itself.

Similarly, movement in floors can produce corresponding cracks in liquid-applied membranes. Although high-grade asphalt does have considerable flexibility, and can heal minor movement cracks, many house floors, particularly in the 1940s and 1950s, were damp-proofed with thin, weak bituminous screeds of very limited effectiveness. Some modern liquid-applied membranes cure to form a tough, flexible sheet material with greater capacity for elongation than polythene, while other epoxy materials bond sufficiently to the floor to resist water pressure, as well as being strong enough for the direct application of floor finishes.

While an isolated crack in masonry, which also causes a local DPC failure, can often be simply repaired, widespread DPC failure through ageing warrants a replacement strategy.

Alteration

Many 'DPC failures' are simply due to careless or ill thought-out alterations to the fabric of a house that overcome the DPC by applying porous material 'bridging' from beneath the DPC to above it, so allowing moisture to by-pass the DPC and rise in the wall or floor above. The commonest examples would be in raised ground levels, external rendering, internal plastering or flooring (*see* Fig 16); once an error like this is diagnosed, it can be a relatively simple process to remove the 'bridging' and return the DPC to its role as an effective barrier, without by-passes.

Forming a new opening in a wall, though not in itself DPC bridging, often involves rebuilding to form masonry reveals at each side of the opening to support new lintels: where an existing horizontal DPC has been

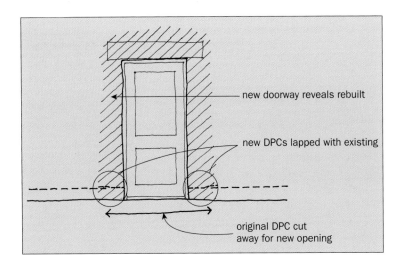

Fig 19   Reinstating DPCs in alteration work.

new doorway reveals rebuilt

new DPCs lapped with existing

original DPC cut away for new opening

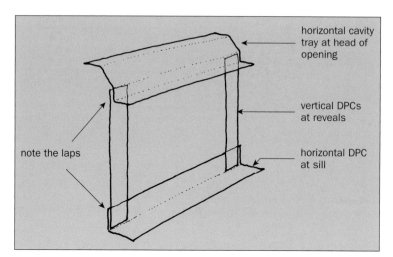

horizontal cavity tray at head of opening

vertical DPCs at reveals

note the laps

horizontal DPC at sill

Fig 20   DPC for protection to an opening in a cavity wall.

cut away, it needs to be carefully reinstated in the new masonry and lapped or bonded with the existing DPC.

Similarly, in cavity wall construction, a new opening's reveals connect the inner and outer leaves of the wall, which can allow both rising and penetrating damp to cross into the inner leaf, so vertical DPCs are needed. The same damp transfer would happen at the head of the opening – gravity-assisted, which is where the cavity tray is inserted to direct any water in the cavity to the outer leaf, usually above the lintel where it can drain out through 'weepholes', and at the sill to protect the wall below. All three types of DPC need to be carefully connected and lapped to shed water outwards. Wall ties are another even more widespread potential route for damp across cavities, which cannot be protected by DPCs: instead they are made with a central twist or 'drip' that discourages water from crossing from outer leaf to inner.

Cavity walls are a tried and tested means of keeping buildings dry but they rely on careful and consistent workmanship: without this, they can be highly vulnerable to damp. The sensible principle in minor alterations is to examine how the house was built and – providing it was built successfully – follow the same details in the alteration work – though the Building Inspector may not always agree! There is no virtue in altering a traditionally built solid wall as though it was a cavity wall, since DPCs will have a purely local effect (but *see* Chapter 3 for measures appropriate against penetrating damp).

Careless Construction

Amongst other problems, careless construction can lead to such a build-up of mortar droppings at the base of a cavity wall that 'hidden bridges' are formed, which allow moisture to reach the inner leaf of the wall: unless the poor workmanship has been unusually consistent, this fault will tend to produce patchy or intermittent areas of rising damp along a wall.

Similar effects can be produced by poorly fitted DPCs, inadequately jointed or fitted slightly out of line with a wall, so that finishes or pointing bridge over them, or simply not connected or sealed to the floor DPM. Where DPCs appear to be visibly intact and unbridged, the appearance of rising damp can be caused by condensation at floor level providing a moisture source, which then rises up the inner leaf and plaster (*see* Chapter 4).

Dampness, like the rest of nature, is nothing to do with fairness or just deserts: the shoddiest workmanship in one house will be enough to keep it dry, whereas in a damp-prone building, the most professional of builders may be caught out. So, in considering solutions to rising-damp problems, it is important first to establish the degree of dampness and then to resolve what sort of result is acceptable.

Absence

Since damp-proof courses were progressively introduced to new house building from late in the nineteenth century, it follows that between 10 and 15 per cent of

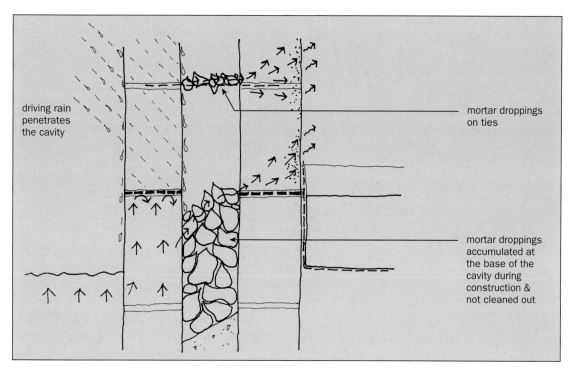

driving rain
penetrates
the cavity

mortar droppings
on ties

mortar droppings
accumulated at
the base of the
cavity during
construction &
not cleaned out

Fig 21   Mortar droppings allow damp to cross the cavity.

the nation's homes dating from earlier periods were built without DPCs – perhaps three million or so. Although this may well mean that most of them are technically subject to rising damp, the damp-proofing industry has treated perhaps a majority of them – the industry has been too diverse for records to have been kept. Although some of the rest are doubtless subject to significant rising-damp problems, and likely to be treated in due course, many others are inhabited by people content with their circumstances, who by a combination of geography, geology, hydrology and appropriate household management, manage to live successfully without DPCs.

How Much Damp is Acceptable?

Modern expectations and the theories of modern construction direct us towards the absolute 'no damp', which is somewhat ironic when we realize how much moisture we 'discharge' within our homes while washing, cooking and simply breathing – typically between 12 and 20ltr per person per day. There is also the anomaly, common enough in centrally heated

houses, of 'humidification': deliberate introduction of dampness to the dessicated internal atmosphere, so as to render it pleasanter and healthier.

For most modern houses on reasonably level ground, the conventionally detailed DPCs and DPMs work well and straightforwardly; repairs to occasional failures or making good after faulty alterations are usually quite simple once the problem is diagnosed – providing that rising damp is the only culprit; though, for long-standing faults, dealing with the aftermath of drying-out and making good finishes can be more difficult than repairing the actual damp fault (Chapter 6 deals with this).

Traditional construction, on the other hand, is less clearly defined; materials and components tend to work together to varying degrees of effectiveness. Solid walls without DPCs are likely to suffer from rising damp and penetrating damp to some degree, depending on many factors such as the dampness of the site and the quality and condition of the materials. In mild cases, where traditional damp-tolerant finishes like lime plasters remain or where wainscoting or panelling at low level conceals the damp, the occupants may well be quite content, or they may have a situation where improvement is desirable but wholesale 'treatment' is too disruptive or costly to be acceptable. A typical example of this situation might be an old house with solid masonry walls and stone-flagged floors, with the latter especially adding to its character (and value). With neither DPCs in its walls nor DPMs below its floors, the house may well exhibit symptoms of rising damp and these could well have increased in severity over the last half-century, perhaps with the replacement of old lime plaster with less damp-tolerant gypsum plasters, or even simply with redecoration to walls using vinyl emulsions, oil paints or vinyl-faced papers.

Conventional remedial solutions to the damp walls would include a new damp course, perhaps an injected chemical DPC, whose installers would probably require internal and external walls stripped of their plaster and refinished to at least a metre above the level of the new DPC. In so far as the new DPC is effective in the walls, it may well produce a marked *increase* in damp in the stone floors, as the walls lose their role wicking moisture away into the atmosphere. The logical solution to this would be to take up the stone flags and relay them over a new DPM (and insulation), so the overall cost and disruption is extremely high. For more severe cases, this may prove to be the best solution, provided the walling material is appropriate to the new DPC. If the house were Listed, of course, this approach might not be permitted. In historic houses, particularly those of the seventeenth or earlier centuries, there is a risk in removing old plaster that historic decorations or wall paintings, often concealed by subsequent 'modernizing decorations', may be destroyed, so careful exploration should precede removal and expert assistance may be needed.

Less drastic measures to simply reduce the problem, rather than eliminate it, could include: laying land drains around the house at foundation level to lower a high water-table; checking the state of drains, particularly rainwater drains and soak-aways to ensure they are not contributing to the damp; and renovating wall surfaces inside and out to replace moisture-sensitive, salt-laden finishes with more tolerant and vapour-permeable ones, like lime render or plaster and traditional or 'green' paints.

This scenario exemplifies the 'intolerance zone' for rising damp: householders tend to object when it damages finishes, most typically when it causes paint and plaster to distort, peel and decay, or when it causes secondary effects like mould or timber decay. So, in considering remedial action, it is important to balance the measures taken with the need and the desired result: rectifying faults in generally effective damp courses and membranes in modern construction makes sense, whereas 'total solutions' to naturally damp traditional construction may not.

REMEDIAL MEASURES FOR RISING DAMP

These can be usefully considered in three groups: the preventers, the reducers and the concealers. Each has its place and there is no universally appropriate solution

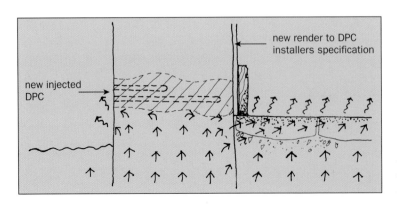

Fig 22   New DPC in walls diverts rising damp into the adjacent stone floor.

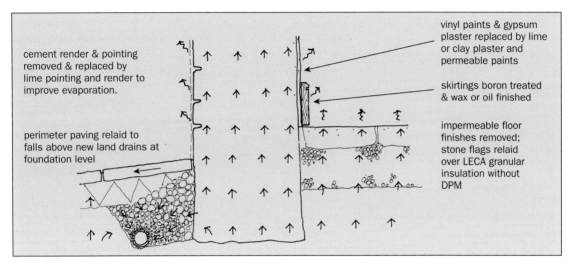

cement render & pointing removed & replaced by lime pointing and render to improve evaporation.

perimeter paving relaid to falls above new land drains at foundation level

vinyl paints & gypsum plaster replaced by lime or clay plaster and permeable paints

skirtings boron treated & wax or oil finished

impermeable floor finishes removed; stone flags relaid over LECA granular insulation without DPM

Fig 23   Integrated measures to minimize rising damp and mitigate its effects.

to any problem: once we put houses together with their sites and their occupants, virtually every case is unique.

The Preventers

These are the measures that block the passage of rising damp, whether as membranes or as damp-proof courses. They include sophisticated technological solutions to reduce the porosity of construction materials chemically and electrically, as well as simple barriers inserted across walls or applied to floors as tanking. Although their theoretical effect is complete, their actual performance – particularly in the case of chemical, electrical and evaporative DPCs – varies with the suitability of the construction and the quality of the workmanship. This may not matter because a partially effective measure may still be sufficient to reduce the rising damp to an acceptable degree but it is important for us to have the right expectations.

Physical DPC Insertion

This is the only fully reliable and potentially permanent method of retro-fitting a DPC, but it is a slow and laborious process and therefore relatively expensive except in the thinnest and simplest walls. The method is to cut through the full thickness of the wall, including both internal and any external finishes, to form a gap wide enough to allow the insertion of

both DPC material and dense mortar above and below it. To allow the wall to maintain its structural stability, the cutting is done in short lengths, typically of around one metre, and can be alternated in a similar way to underpinning foundations. The installer's skill and judgement is needed to assess the structural suitability of the wall and to carry out the work with a minimum of damage, dust and disruption. In some cases, a structural engineer's advice may be needed before the work is done to confirm whether the wall is suitable and to agree the distribution and length of the cuts.

Particular care needs to be taken to remove vulnerable services, such as electric cables and pipes, from walls and to avoid or minimize damage to historic fabric, internally or externally. Materials for insertion include the full range of the tougher flexible DPCs in plastics, metals and 'sandwiches' of both, as well as rigid slate and metals, especially for historic buildings.

In making good after the DPC is inserted, it is important to avoid bridging over the new DPC, just as in new construction, and the same care is needed to connect the DPC to ground-floor DPMs. Bedding mortars need to be sufficiently dense to bear the weight of the wall, and usually include chemical additives to improve workability and strength; dryish mixes are used to allow dense packing and minimize shrinkage.

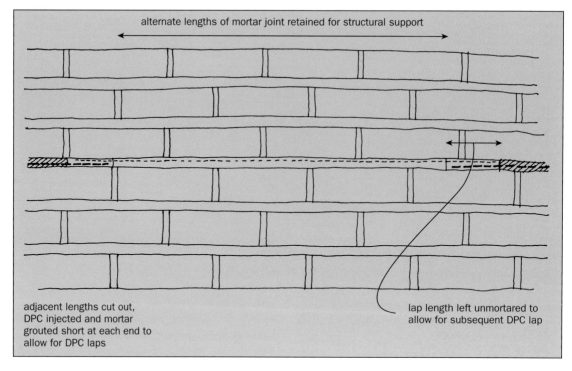

alternate lengths of mortar joint retained for structural support

adjacent lengths cut out,
DPC injected and mortar
grouted short at each end to
allow for DPC laps

lap length left unmortared to
allow for subsequent DPC lap

Fig 24   Alternating lengths of DPC cuts allow structural stability to be retained.

Chemical Injection

These are the largest group of remedial damp-proof course systems offered by specialist contractors and include the only systems whose installation is covered under a British Standard (BS 6576: 1985) and, in some cases, by an Agrement Certificate. Damp-proof 'injection' is normally carried out by specialist contractors: their trade association, the British Wood Preserving and Damp-Proofing Association (01332 225100) can provide helpful advice.

The fluids used are based mainly on silicons or aluminium stearates, injected under high pressure, low pressure or simply gravity-fed ('transfused') into the wall construction. The use of solvent carriers is being generally phased out for environmental reasons and because the control of the chemical damp-repellents, in both distribution through the damp wall and retention in the pore structure, has been better developed in water-borne solutions.

Holes are drilled into the thickness of the wall to saturate a zone usually around 75–150mm (3–6in) high at approximately 150mm (6in) above external

ground level, at various centres and depths, to allow for the saturation of the wall material. For more porous stone or brickwork, holes can be drilled into the bricks or stones; with a consistent mortar or, for aesthetic or historical reasons, it may be preferred to drill into the mortar joints.

The skill in carrying out the work lies largely in judging the appropriate frequency and depth of the drilling according to the wall material, and the application of the correct quantities of fluid to ensure full saturation. The injected damp course has to be continuous through all walling, inside and out, that does not already include a DPC. Vertical injected DPCs can be used to separate treated walls from adjacent retaining walls that may need tanking, or from adjacent buildings that are not similarly treated; without such vertical injection, rising damp from the adjacent wall or building can simply spread sideways into the treated wall *above* the new DPC (Fig 26).

In consistent walling material and with good workmanship, injection is usually very successful at forming a sufficiently non-porous zone in the wall to act as a

Fig 25   Injected DPC installation by transfusion into the mortar joints. (Peter Cox)

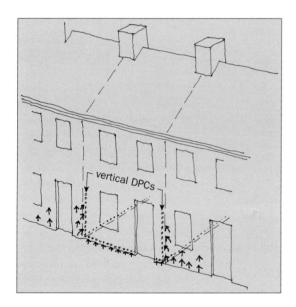

Fig 26   Vertical DPCs injected to prevent rising damp spreading from adjacent untreated walls.

barrier to rising moisture. Typically appropriate wall materials would be solid and well-mortared brickwork or stonework of consistent porosity. Inappropriate construction would be random masonry where stone or mortar are inconsistent and may include voids – although it may be feasible to grout such walling before

injecting the DPC – or where some or all of the material may be impervious, such as flint or overburnt or engineering brick. In theory, such materials should work as damp courses in themselves and, when carefully and consistently laid in waterproof or damp-resistant mortars, they work very well; but when they occur randomly in otherwise porous construction, they disrupt the formation of a consistent chemical damp-course.

The task also becomes more difficult as the wall thickness increases and the chances of consistent drilling and saturation are reduced. Traditional random rubble stone walls are particularly difficult to treat because the thick walls are normally built as an inner and outer skin of irregular stone in weak mortar, with the core of the wall backfilled with stone debris and mortar as construction proceeds; this core-fill material is often of very poor quality and frequently includes voids, making the injection of it unpredictable and its damp-proofing unreliable. Although air-filled voids do not in themselves transmit moisture, they tend to prevent the even absorption of the damp-proofing fluid. Damp-proofing pastes and creams can be injected in lieu of fluids and may perform better in irregular walling with voids.

Electrical Damp-Courses
Electro-osmotic damp courses are installed by some firms as an alternative to chemical injection; they

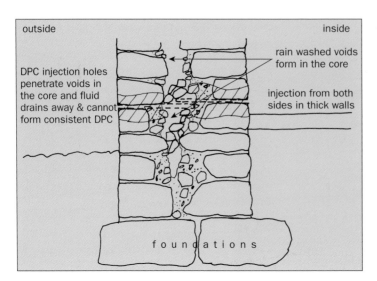

Fig 27   Void problems for DPC injection in rubble walls.

work by introducing a positive electrical charge into the masonry at the base of the wall to counteract capillary action on the rising moisture. They are installed by inserting anodes of corrosion-resistant metals, such as copper, titanium, etc., into holes drilled into the wall at close intervals – typically 400mm (16in) apart – connected in a ring circuit by a cable set into a 'chase' or groove in the wall, usually at a mortar joint in the masonry. The ring circuit is wired to the mains via a transformer to deliver a small positive charge. Just like chemical damp-courses, these work best in consistent materials and will be disadvantaged by irregular construction and voids.

Evaporative Damp-Courses
These have a long history but arguably could be classified as 'reducers' rather than 'preventers' since they work by enhancing the evaporative potential of the wall immediately above ground level and not by forming a barrier as such. However, they have been

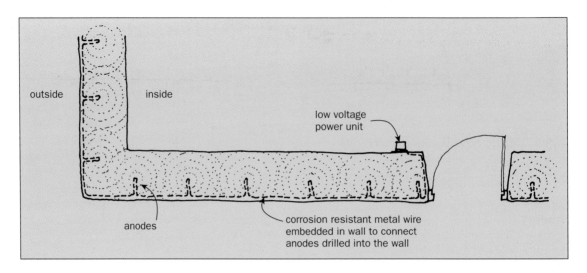

Fig 28   Electro-osmotic DPCs electrically charge wall material to counteract capillary action.

marketed, with guarantees, in the same way as other systems to 'cure' rising damp problems, and since they share with other systems some success by partial prevention of rising damp leading to effective reduction of symptoms, they can be considered alongside preventers.

The various patent methods share the principle of inserting a row of open-pored ceramic tubes or pots into the wall, vented to the outside, that provide an easier route for the evaporation of rising damp than through interior finishes. The tube or pot is capped externally to prevent rain penetration and occupation by insects, and it is set in place in the wall using a moisture-permeable mortar.

First sold as the Narben tube system in the 1930s, which achieved a notable success at the palace of Versailles, it was taken up by Protim Services in the UK and marketed until the 1960s, when the reliability and cost of chemical systems improved. Royal Doulton marketed their own version into the 1970s. Currently, a more elaborately designed ceramic pot system, developed in Holland and known as the Schrijver System, is marketed by one company nationally who offer 30-year guarantees and stress an advantage of the system as avoiding the need for internal replastering; although it is difficult to see how this method would have such an advantage over other systems, particularly where hygroscopic salts have accumulated at the plaster surfaces. The very process of stimulating evaporation would appear to be subject to long-term degradation by the accumulation of salts: just as these tend to build up in internal plasters, clogging the pores and causing the moisture to rise higher, it would be surprising if salts accumulating in the ceramic pots or tubes would not gradually decrease their effectiveness.

Although the Dutch system's ceramic chambers are more sophisticated in their design to induce airflow, condensation and moisture removal, they do not have the simple option of various lengths, as in the tubular systems to suit different wall thicknesses, and, like any such system, they are very dependent on local wind and weather conditions. However, the principle of promoting evaporation from a damp wall is a good one since it is less likely to cause damp problems elsewhere – in adjacent floors or in adjoining houses, for example – by preventing the damp from rising in the walls.

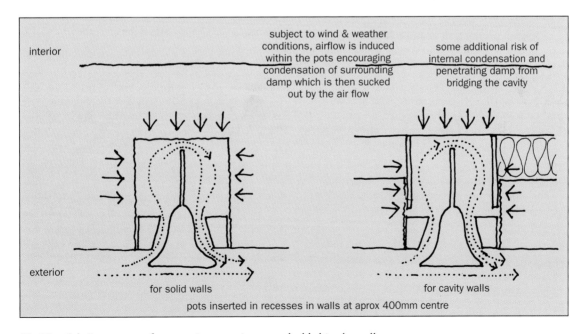

Fig 29   Schrijver system of evaporative ceramic pots embedded in the wall.

Accompanying Wall Treatments

For most rising-damp treatments, especially those offering guarantees, the specification will normally include complete and thorough removal of internal finishes to at least 1m (3ft 3in) above external ground level and their replacement with a render mix to the specialists' specification, typically including a salt-inhibiting additive in a cement and sharp sand mix, often at a ratio of 1:3. However, the Building Research Establishment's Digest 245 suggests that 1:3 mixes are too strong and too vapour-proof for most situations, and that renders should be both highly vapour-permeable and weaker than the background masonry, which means that a more appropriate mix might be 1:6 or weaker. Although, the replacement of salt-contaminated plasters is a necessary part of a thorough treatment of rising damp, so as to prevent the ongoing appearance of symptoms from the period prior to the installation of the damp course, the use of strong cement renders has no logic except as a belt and braces approach to waterproofing, on the basis that if the DPC does not work properly, the cement render will probably be sufficiently waterproof anyway. The major flaw in this argument is that strong cement render mixes are notoriously brittle and prone to shrinkage cracks; once cracked, their 'back-up waterproofing role' is negated. So, unless the walls being treated are built of dense concrete or engineering brick, replacement render mixes should be nearer 1:6 or 1:8 than 1:3, and follow the BRE and BS guidelines. With the weaker, more vapour-permeable mixes, there is less chance of the residual rising damp – or any moisture that gets past a partially effective DPC – being forced upwards in the wall to cause damage to finishes above the level of new finishes. Householders should be suspicious of DPC installers whose specifications call for strong cement mixes, regardless of the background.

The removal and replacement of plaster is by far the most disruptive part of the DPC installation since, in most cases, the DPC installations are carried out externally. The exceptions to this are for interior walls, for very thick external walls and especially for chimney breasts, which even though forming part of an external wall, are likely to need treatment from both sides.

Although damp-proof specialists will be able to carry out treatment without stripping and replacing finishes, they are very unlikely to issue guarantees for such work because the probability of symptoms appearing from the residual moisture in the wall or from salts accumulated in the plaster is very high.

In many cases, installation of a damp course and issue of a guarantee will be a condition of a purchaser's mortgage, so there may be no choice but to undergo the full treatment and the disruption involved. Where there is no such compulsion, householders with lesser rising-damp problems may choose to save both cost and disruption, accepting the possibility that symptoms may recur, and the future risk that a potential purchaser's surveyor may identify the installed DPC as defective – or at least unguaranteed – and thereby seek to reduce the sale price of the house.

Accompanying Tanking

The other stipulation from DPC installers is that, where their new DPC, usually at around 150mm (6in) above external ground level, is installed above internal floor levels, there should be 'tanking' (a waterproof treatment to the face of the wall) from the DPC down to floor level or to connect with a DPM below the floor, if there is one. This treatment can take several forms but most often will involve a basecoat waterproof render to the stripped wall followed by three coats of a liquid waterproof coating, either bitumen or rubber based, with the top coat dressed with sharp sand while still wet to form a key for the application of render and plaster. If a wall is sound and fair-faced, in evenly pointed brickwork for example, there may be no need for the basecoat of render, but most walls in these circumstances are too rough to take reliable application of waterproofing and need the basecoat render to smooth the surface and close up the crevices that would otherwise form a weakness in the waterproofing coats. This process and these locations at the base of the wall are most vulnerable to poor workmanship; conscientious preparation and thorough application of both the base render and the waterproofing coats are essential for success.

Sheet-tanking materials adhered to the wall may be used instead of liquids but they tend to be more costly and to require more consistent backgrounds, and even more careful workmanship, than liquid tanking. Polythene sheet DPMs may be extended from the floor to meet the DPC level and adhered to the wall, but they are more vulnerable to damage than

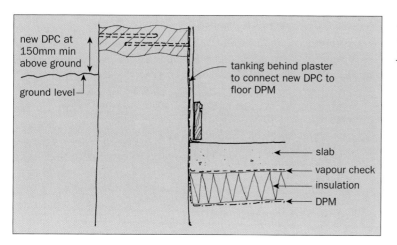

Fig 30   Floors below ground level: linking DPC to DPM in floor.

proprietary sheet-tanking and less effective at self-healing around punctures than liquid applications.

In subsequent making good of finishes, particularly replacement of skirting boards, care needs to be taken not to puncture the new tanking. In most cases, skirtings and other low-level joinery can be glued in place rather than screwed or nailed. If this is not possible, the tanking can be extended into pockets for fixing blocks or holes drilled for wallplugs and screws can be injected with a mastic compatible with the

tanking before the plugs are inserted. Tanking is further discussed in Chapter 3.

Damp-Proofing To Floors
Rising damp in floors does not necessarily accompany the problem in walls, though it is often linked to it and may well be exacerbated by the installation of DPCs in walls, just as the reverse may happen with a newly waterproofed floor causing rising damp to become a serious problem in the surrounding walls.

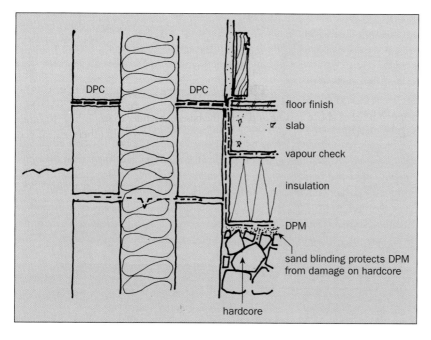

Fig 31   DPM in current solid ground floor.

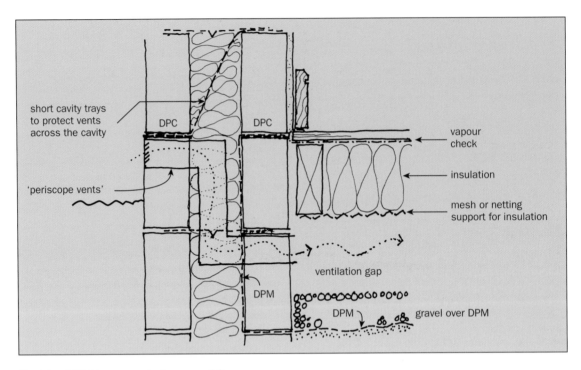

short cavity trays
to protect vents
across the cavity

DPC

DPC

vapour
check

insulation

mesh or netting
support for insulation

'periscope vents'

DPM

ventilation gap

DPM

gravel over DPM

Fig 32   DPM in current timber ground floor.

There are two main types of ground floors in housing: the solid earth-based floor and the suspended floor, usually of timber in traditional housing, though increasingly of precast concrete beams and blocks in the last 50 years. In modern construction, both types will have both DPMs and insulation but traditionally, both types of floor would have neither.

Suspended Ground Floors   Suspended timber floors relied on a ventilated sub-floor void to keep the timber joists and floor boards reasonably dry and free of decay: before the advent of fitted carpets, this made such floors often cold and draughty; even with them, draughts and heat loss remain considerable. Either as a direct result of attempts to reduce draughts, or through careless alteration of garden levels, many sub-floor vents get blocked, which can lead to substantial dampness and timber decay in the floor structure. Also contributing to timber decay in the floor joists is rising damp in the 'sleeper walls' or external walls supporting them; pre-twentieth century housing is unlikely to include any form of DPC below floor joists.

Ideally, new DPCs are inserted at the level below floor joists but ground levels are often too high for this, which means that a DPC installed at or above the level of a timber floor can make its situation significantly worse by increasing the levels of rising damp just where the joists are built into the walls.

If there is any question as to the effectiveness of the sub-floor ventilation, and particularly if there is already decay in the floor, it may be necessary to replace the timber floor with a solid concrete one with its DPM connected to the new wall DPCs. A possible alternative is to cut back the timber joists from the external walls and support them on new sleeper walls over DPCs; any existing sleeper walls can be fitted with DPCs under the joists at the same time. Thorough provision for ventilation should be made and the floor should be insulated between the joists with a polythene vapour-check laid over the joists before the boards are replaced, all of which tends to be more labour-intensive, and therefore costly, than a new solid floor.

Suspended concrete ground floors – in houses, virtually always made of pre-cast concrete planks or

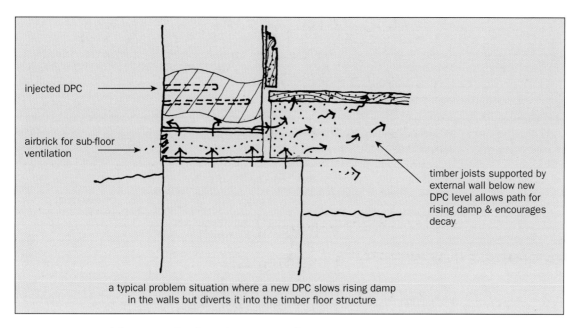

injected DPC

airbrick for sub-floor ventilation

timber joists supported by external wall below new DPC level allows path for rising damp & encourages decay

a typical problem situation where a new DPC slows rising damp in the walls but diverts it into the timber floor structure

Fig 33   Damp and decay in timber floor after DPC installation.

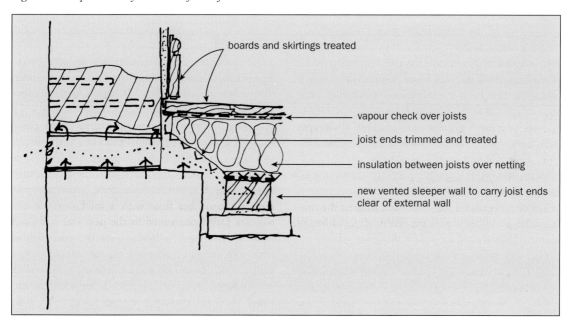

boards and skirtings treated

vapour check over joists

joist ends trimmed and treated

insulation between joists over netting

new vented sleeper wall to carry joist ends clear of external wall

Fig 34   Remedial work to timber floor at DPC installation.

beams with concrete block or hollow clay block infill, sometimes grouted solid and sometimes laid 'dry' – have been used increasingly by house-builders since the 1950s, especially for housing on sloping sites or over made-up ground, where conventional hardcore and *in situ*, ground-bearing concrete slabs would have been too costly or too unreliable. As an element of relatively modern house-building subject to building regulations, these floors generally prove more reliable in terms of damp than their traditional timber counterparts; their concrete components also have the advantage over timber of being unaffected by damp. However, they do not lend themselves to insulation in the same simple way as timber-joisted floors and can give rise to serious condensation problems (*see* Chapter 4).

Some later designs substituted polystyrene blocks for the concrete or clay block infill, and one design included interlocking polystyrene slabs that insulated below the beams to avoid cold bridging. An alternative approach to solving the floor-insulation requirement is to overlay the beams and blocks with insulation slabs and a 'floating floor' of chipboard or similar sheets: to avoid condensation problems, it is important that such floors include a vapour check above the insulation (*see* Chapter 4).

Solid Ground Floors   In the simplest cases, a sound, solid floor suffering from damp, whether it is concrete or some other material, may have its finishes removed and a liquid DPM applied – preferably water-based rather than solvent-based for health and environmental reasons – usually in two or three coats. If finishes are to be replaced directly, this will need to be a tough epoxy material suitable for direct loading; otherwise, a protective cement-sand screed, usually at least 50mm (2in) thick, is laid over the new DPM, which obviously raises the finished floor level by at least that amount. This process will leave no opportunity for insulating the floor, nor, for example, for installing under-floor heating, which can be one of the comfort and environmental bonuses of having to damp-proof or renew a floor. To improve matters in these ways, or perhaps because the existing solid floor is in poor condition, it may be necessary to take up the floor completely, excavate its base and start again.

In order to benefit from the available thermal mass of the floor slab – especially in these times of global warming – it is usually best to insulate below the slab. Unless the sub-floor material is unusually hard – the Building Inspector will advise – it will be necessary to excavate this material to allow for a scalpings or hard-core base, blinded with sand, on which the polythene sheet DPM is laid, with any necessary joints double-folded, over which the insulation is laid – typically a foam-insulation board of the appropriate density,

followed by a second polythene sheet, serving both as vapour check and to keep the concrete out of the insulation – followed by the concrete slab, usually 100mm (4in) thick and unreinforced (incorporating the under-floor heating pipes if these are required), and the final floor finish (*see* Fig 10). In the case of traditional floors, such as stone slabs, paving bricks, quarry tiles, parquet or similar, which may need to be retained, these are carefully lifted, set aside and relaid as the final floor finish, allowing for the extra depth needed. It may be preferred to relay floors exactly as they were, in which case, slabs can be individually numbered and the floor photographed before it is taken up. Both the DPM and the vapour check should be dressed up the wall to connect with the level of the DPC or with any tanking applied below it.

The Reducers

This category of measures does not offer guarantees and so may not be sufficient to satisfy mortgage lenders. However, these measures do offer (some) less disruptive and simpler approaches to the problems of rising damp, which may be more in sympathy with traditional construction and particularly appropriate to historic buildings in some cases.

Lowering the Water-Table

This is clearly not an option available in all cases (for example, where ground adjacent to the house is not within the same ownership) but, where feasible, the process can be relatively simple and sometimes low in cost. A typical measure to reduce rising and penetrating damp can be to lower ground levels immediately adjacent to an affected wall, though rising damp can persist despite this unless a substantial set-back is achieved.

Introducing land drainage at foundation level can be substantially more effective, particularly where foundations are significantly below floor level, with the advantage that external ground levels can be retained (*see* Fig 23). Drainage should not be lower than the base of foundations unless the substructure is impervious, probably rock, since reducing water levels in shrinkable sub-soils can cause serious subsidence. The details of such land drains are straightforward. Ideally, access should be allowed for rodding

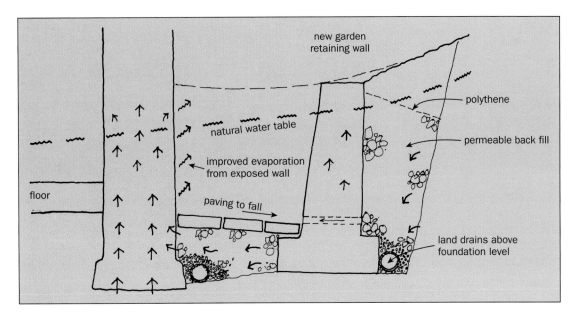

Fig 35   Lowering external ground levels to reduce rising damp.

but with correct detailing, such drainage should last for decades without maintenance.

Changing Finishes

Serious rising damp can be too much for any finishes but there are many, perhaps the majority of cases, where the primary problem is in fact the damage to finishes. It is also the case that over the last century, there has been a steady decline in the use of damp-tolerant finishes, paralleling the increased use of damp-proof construction detailing.

The earlier changes were the gradual replacement of lime renders and plasters by cement renders and later gypsum plasters. Lime mixes are significantly more vapour-permeable than cement mixes, and both lime and cement-based plasters are markedly more moisture-tolerant than gypsum-based plasters. Gypsum – calcium hydroxide – reacts with water and this weakens both *in situ* plasters and gypsum plasterboards, so that with persistent damp they break down and can no longer retain paint finishes.

In the last fifty years, the loss of damp-tolerance has been compounded by the widespread use of vinyl emulsion paints, which, despite their other virtues, are much less vapour-permeable than non-vinyl emulsions, traditional distempers and limewashes. It is significant that 'trade emulsions' used by professional decorators, often over new plaster, are almost vinyl-free, and even where new plaster has been well-dried, it is recommended that its first decoration is carried out using non-vinyl paints. Other finishes, such as oil-based paints, vinyl-faced wallpapers or ceramic tiles, are likely to be even less permeable than vinyl emulsions; where such finishes are applied over gypsum plasters to damp walls, they tend to cause a moisture build-up in the plaster and progressive breakdown; where applied over more moisture-tolerant cement or lime-based renders, they encourage the damp to rise further up the wall.

Traditional solutions to serious rising damp included dado panelling in timber, which, by allowing an airspace between the wall and panelling or boarding, detached the timber from the worst of the damp and produced a paintable or polishable wooden finish that was also more robust and hard-wearing than traditional soft limewashes or distempers. With more serious damp levels, the timber in turn – particularly the support battening – tends to suffer progressive decay, particularly where there is no significant airflow to remove the moisture.

Fig 36   Delamination in stone floor slabs due to salts from rising damp.

Permeable Floor Finishes

Traditional ground-floor finishes tend to be both tough and permeable; for example, (most) stone flags and brick paving, rammed clay and chalk, and timber. Later tile floors, particularly quarry tiles, were less permeable. Even where stone or brick is laid directly onto the earth, they can produce a consistently vapour-permeable and moisture-tolerant hard-wearing floor finish that coexists with rising damp; though timber floors are usually relatively short-lived unless well-ventilated, as described above. Better traditional detailing laid such finishes over a layer of gravel, which significantly reduces the direct absorption of ground moisture into the floor material. Such details without DPMs remain the norm for new floors in existing buildings in some parts of Europe.

Later 'improvements', such as sealing stone or tile floors or overlaying them with sheet flooring materials, may produce a short-term gain in modernity and cleanability, but this will be at the expense of trapping rising moisture within the floor and potentially causing decay, or of diverting rising damp into the surrounding walls.

Conversely, existing situations can be improved by stripping away overlaid finishes and restoring the original vapour-permeability; hard-wearing yet permeable wax and oil finishes are available for stone, tile,

etc., and for timber floors, if the plain surfaces needs resealing after stripping. For stone and brick floors, it is important that the grouting of joints is done with a mortar both weaker and more permeable than the flooring material itself, which encourages the passage of moisture through the joints rather than through the slabs or bricks. Any salt migration tends, therefore, to be concentrated in the joints rather than the slabs, where it can be readily removed in the course of minor repointing, rather than causing delamination or decay in the surface of the slabs themselves.

The Concealers

Covering up problems of rising damp must have been the earliest of solutions, long before the knowledge and the technology were available to propose 'cures'. Done for the right reasons, without subterfuge, it can be a perfectly satisfactory long-term solution, but it is important to understand the implications of this approach.

Panelling and Tapestries

Traditional concealment tended to be for aesthetic reasons and the cladding of damp walls with various forms of panelling, in timber or fabrics, for example, relied on some degree of air separation – as well as the permeability of the panelling material – to minimize decay. Since there is no attempt made to *prevent* the rising damp entering the house, merely to conceal its effects, the method is not satisfactory in severe cases because humidity tends to be too high and the musty smell of damp too unpleasant; the concealing cladding also tends to decay. In moderate cases, however, the results can be perfectly satisfactory, especially if provision can be made for air circulation behind the concealing material.

Lath and Platon

The classic material developed for this purpose was Newtonite Lath, a corrugated pitch-fibre sheet material invented by John Newton in 1937, which was simply nailed to damp walls with the corrugations vertical, then plastered over with discreet open gaps left at ceiling and skirting, which allowed sufficient air circulation to prevent the build-up of damp damage. In many cases, this material has been used as an unventilated tanking and to resist mild dampness sufficiently for the survival of plaster and paint, it has worked well.

In the last few decades, the same principle has been embodied in plastic 'platon' sheet materials – similar in form to the multi-recessed linings of chocolate boxes – produced by a number of manufacturers and used for 'diversionary tanking' (*see* Chapter 3), as well as for airflow drylining.

Drylinings

Simple drylining, normally of gypsum plasterboard, or sometimes hardboard, fixed to walls on battens, has become the commonest and cheapest form of concealment – or 'upgrading', depending on your point of view – of defective wall surfaces generally, including symptoms of rising damp. The inclusion of a waterproof building paper or, more recently, polythene sheet against the wall reduces the absorption of damp into the house and the tendency of the fixing battens to decay, but encourages rising damp to rise higher, particularly with the less permeable exterior wall finishes, such as strong cement renders. Any drylining in damp areas should be done with 'moisture-resistant plasterboard' to reduce the likelihood of gypsum breakdown. Better quality drylinings increasingly incorporate insulation either as a separate layer between fixing battens or in a laminated combination with the plasterboard which reduces fixing costs.

Where there is any significant damp, it is advisable for the insulation material to be non-absorptive, usually a closed cell, rigid foam, and in all situations for the laminate to incorporate a vapour check on the warm side of the insulation to discourage interstitial condensation (*see* Chapter 4).

Laminated insulation board drylinings – as well as plain plasterboard – can also be fixed to walls without

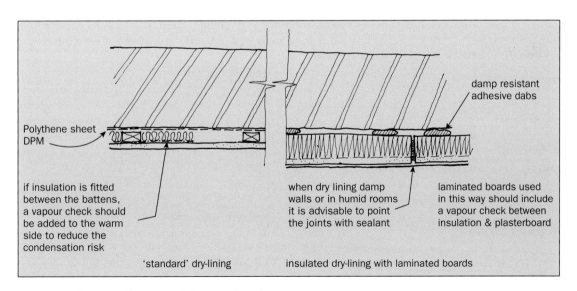

Polythene sheet DPM

damp resistant adhesive dabs

if insulation is fitted between the battens, a vapour check should be added to the warm side to reduce the condensation risk

when dry lining damp walls or in humid rooms it is advisable to point the joints with sealant

laminated boards used in this way should include a vapour check between insulation & plasterboard

'standard' dry-lining   insulated dry-lining with laminated boards

Fig 37   Drylining walls to conceal damp and insulate.

battens using 'dabs' – trowelled or gunned dollops of adhesive at regular intervals to support and adhere the drylining with an airspace against the wall. The standard gypsum-based dab adhesives should not be used in damp conditions; water-resistant versions and cement-based alternatives are available.

Tanking – lining construction with a fully waterproof pressure-resistant layer – is a more extreme form of concealment, which is seldom used to keep out rising damp alone, due to its high costs, but more widely to waterproof retaining walls against penetrating damp; this is dealt with in Chapter 3.

Small areas of lower key tanking to connect floor DPMs to wall DPCs above floor level have already been described above.

The Gradient of Permeability

An important principle in all forms of external wall construction and treatment, but especially critical in the process of drylining and concealing damp, is to achieve – and maintain – a gradient of permeability that follows the temperature gradient from inside to out: the outer layers of the wall should be more permeable than the inner surfaces, so that as condensation occurs in the colder layers, moisture is easily carried away to external air (*see* Fig 14). The more damp there is in the wall itself – as opposed to moisture migrating from the interior – the more complex the situation becomes and the more risk there is in concealing, rather than preventing or reducing, rising damp.

As we shall see in Chapter 4, condensation is not always so predictable and the gradients can sometimes be reversed, which just emphasizes the need for appropriate solutions: correctly detailed concealment of mild rising damp is perfectly reasonable but more serious cases require more thorough and open solutions.

CHAPTER 3

Penetrating Damp

Penetrating damp is the most obvious type of dampness and although the source of this moisture is obvious – rain, snow, floods – it does not mean that its route into our houses is easily found and blocked. The forces that bring this water into a house are gravity and wind, of which gravity is the easier to follow and to combat; wind does almost unbelievable things with water, frequently defying gravity in the process, and, because it is intermittent and infinitely variable, in both force and direction, it can be extremely difficult to defeat.

Every part of the 'envelope' of a house is vulnerable: the roofs and walls especially but also the ground floors in a few circumstances. Openings and joints in our house surfaces are particularly at risk though these problems are often simply remedied. Some of the most intractable cases of penetrating damp relate to theoretically water-resistant roofs and, especially, walls that have ceased to prevent the passage of moisture.

The ideal in remedying these damp problems is always to shed and divert – to ward off the moisture and then provide it with a safe route away.

DAMP-PENETRATING ROOFS

Pitched roofs are the traditional solution to rain protection in most temperate climates because of their natural 'shedding shape'. In traditional, vernacular housing, higher rainfall tends to produce steeper pitches, although high snowfall has traditionally led to shallower pitches, which safely retain the snow for the winter as an insulating 'blanket'.

It appears that the earliest pitched roofs are thatched: if these are to last, a steep pitch is essential to minimize

saturation and rottin g. Where appropriately thin or easily split stone was available, natural slates were an obvious more permanent roofing. Once houses could be built to carry their weight, fired clay and finally synthetic tiles (concrete, resin, rubber) were the industrial successor to slates and thatch, which in their more sophisticated weathering designs have allowed progressively lower pitches, down to as low as 12 degrees.

Although lead and, to a much lesser extent, copper, zinc and stainless-steel sheet roofs are still widespread on our grander historic buildings, especially on churches, it is only within the last century that sheet materials, principally metals and fibre cements, usually in a profiled form such as corrugated sheeting, have made some inroads into house roofing in the UK. However, they have failed to match the traditional appeal of slates and tiles, to the extent that pressed steel 'sheets of tiles' are marketed for the lightweight over-cladding of flat roofs to social housing. Smooth sheet-metal roofings on the other hand – usually lead, stainless steel or copper – have made an impact in higher cost, particularly contemporary housing. Lead-sheet roofing also has a long history from Roman times via church roofing and roofing for the rich, to its widespread use for flashings, gutters and small roofs to bays.

Most of the details of different roofing materials follow similar principles, suffer similar faults and are dealt with by similar remedies, but it is worth exploring some of their basic characteristics.

Thatched Roofs

Thatched roofs, from having been the commonest form of roofing in periods of cheap labour, have dwindled to a small minority surviving in rural areas, now frequently protected by listed building status. Both the high cost of labour – now often leading to thatching costs of over £20,000 for a small cottage – and the relatively short life – typically twenty years for wheat straw and thirty to forty years for Norfolk reed – led to the widespread replacement of thatched roofs with tiles or slates, until listed building protection was imposed, increasingly, in the 1960s and 1970s. From a million thatched roofs in the nineteenth century, numbers have dwindled to between 20,000 and 30,000.

Thatch – usually of long straw, combed wheat reed or Norfolk reed – differs from other roof materials in that it is fundamentally not waterproof in either its material or its assembly. The principle of thatching is the ultimate in diversionary tactics: although an individual straw is neither waterproof nor even shaped to protect from weather, by close packing straws at a steep angle, they shed water as effectively as a beaver's fur or a duck's feathers, though – luckily for thatchers – they have neither the integral grease supply nor continuous replacement system provided in nature for long-term weather resistance.

Thatches suffer from progressive decay, as well as from birds' gathering nest material. Remedies involve either full stripping and re-thatching or stripping back the most decayed outer material and building up a thinner layer of new thatch over the retained core.

Like most roofs, thatches are most reliable when simplest in form; complex plans or sections leading to convoluted roof shapes, particularly valleys with their reduced pitches, tend to concentrate run-off and accelerate decay. Pitch is critical to the life of thatch; so whereas thatch at 25 degrees may only last ten or fifteen years, at 50 degrees, a forty-five-year life can be expected. Local areas of lower pitch are usually the first to fail.

Since rain penetration of thatch tends to occur progressively by decay and saturation, it is particularly likely to cause decay in roof timbers, which can be steadily 'fed' with moisture from the absorbent

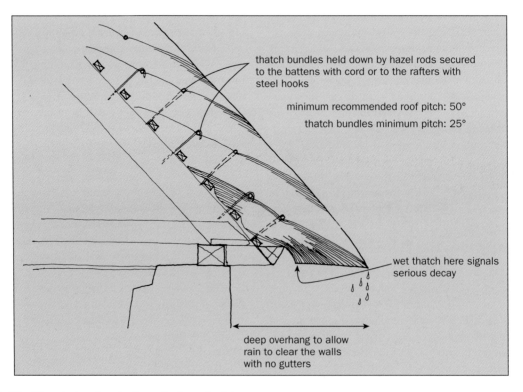

Fig 38   Thatched roofs – the fur or feather principle.

rotting straw. It is also the case that thatch decay accelerates: once the surface begins to break down, the rate of absorption increases, promoting further decay until the roof profile itself subsides, furthering both water retention and rot. Depressions in the thatch or depressed strips down the slope are signs of serious decay, as is wet thatch close to the wall face at the eaves.

Although the number of skilled thatchers declined sharply to a few hundred, there are nearer 2,000 today. Except in the few areas where thatch is still common, particularly in parts of Devon, Dorset and Hampshire, householders may need to use the internet rather than local reputation to find thatchers. There are County Thatchers Associations and a helpful website [www.thatch.org] run by Leo Wood, a semi-retired master thatcher who offers unbiased advice.

Shingles and Shakes

Shingles and shakes, most often of western red cedar but occasionally of oak or other durable timbers, do have a certain affinity with thatch in that they are grown and harvested rather than manufactured as such. Shingles are sawn tapered 'tiles' of timber, usually 400mm (16in) long (up to 600mm long to special order) and of random widths between 75 and 350mm wide (3 and 14in), laid double-lapped; whereas shakes are heavier and similar in shape but produced by

splitting the timber, producing a less regular and more rustic appearance. However, they differ markedly from thatch, both in their ability to shed water as individual 'tiles of timber' and their typically long life, especially if treated with preservative – up to sixty years in many situations and still going strong. In addition, very low pitches are achievable – down to 14 degrees for shingles in reasonably sheltered situations.

The long life and efficiency of shingles is due partly to the inherent durability and water-resistance of the timbers used: the same high oil content that has made western red cedar a preferred timber for greenhouses, sheds and wall cladding, makes it suitable for shingles. The simple layout and fixing – usually by two stainless steel or bronze nails – allows for sufficient movement and thorough drainage to maximize the integrity of the shingle. Their light weight, as low as 6kg/m^2 – only a tenth of the weight of plain tiles – can allow for reduced roof-structure costs.

Despite these significant advantages, shingles are relatively rare in the UK. The few specialist suppliers have traditionally imported them from Canada and the US, although in recent years, limited supplies of UK-grown western red cedar have become available. John Brash, a leading supplier, has a useful website [www.johnbrash.co.uk] with specifications and general information.

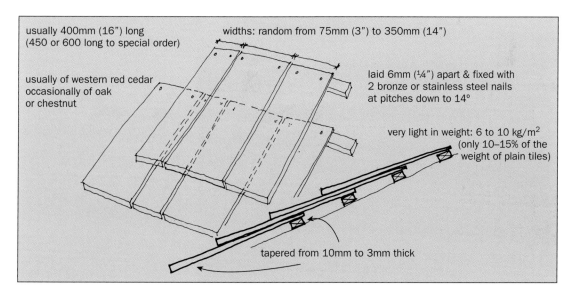

usually 400mm (16") long
(450 or 600 long to special order)

widths: random from 75mm (3") to 350mm (14")

usually of western red cedar
occasionally of oak
or chestnut

laid 6mm (¼") apart & fixed with
2 bronze or stainless steel nails
at pitches down to 14°

very light in weight: 6 to 10 kg/m^2
(only 10–15% of the
weight of plain tiles)

tapered from 10mm to 3mm thick

Fig 39   Shingles and shakes.

Clay and Concrete Tiles

These are usually divided into two categories: single and double lap. Both types tend to be made with 'nibs' at the head to allow the tiles to hook over the battens, though increasingly in the twentieth century, nibs were supplemented by nail fixings, especially at the vulnerable perimeters to roofs, where wind uplift is most likely to dislodge tiles. British Standard BS 5534 1990 describes the appropriate areas for nail-fixing of tiles according to degrees of exposure. Without such nailing, tiles at the most exposed perimeter locations tend to lift in high winds and are occasionally dislodged; large areas can be stripped away in extreme conditions.

Again, the most vulnerable areas tend to be hips, valleys and verges, where tile edges are exposed and where the 'brick bonding' of double-lap tiling and slating leads to the use of half-width tiles and slates with correspondingly inadequate space for fixings. Proper workmanship demands the use of 'one-and-a-half' tiles and slates, made or cut to 1.5 times the standard width, to avoid this problem but their extra cost means they are often omitted. Especially at hips and valleys, this means that small triangular scraps of slate or tile are used to complete the courses and these frequently come adrift.

Single-Lap Tiling

This has only a single thickness of tile over most of the roof surface, except at the head and side laps. The tiles are typically large, often as much as 300mm (12in) wide and 400mm (16in) long. The single cover and large size makes these tiles light (typically around 45kg/m^2 for concrete and 35–40kg/m^2 for clay), quick and relatively cheap to lay, though damage to, or slippage of, a single tile allows rain to penetrate. Traditionally, single-lap tiles have been profiled to improve their individual strength and allow for the side laps. In the UK, the simplest traditional profile is the pantile, with double and triple roman tiles particular to the West country from their manufacturing bases around Bridgewater. Concrete tile makers followed these patterns and gradually diversified in pursuit of lower pitches, increased weather-resistance and manufacturing economies.

Sandtoft have re-introduced both clay and concrete versions of double roman tiles, as well as developing more sophisticated clay pantiles for use at lower pitches.

Double-Lap Plain Tiling

Double-lap or plain tiling has two thicknesses of tile over the whole roof and three at the head laps. Protection of the joints between adjacent tiles is achieved by stepping successive courses of tiles by half a tile's width to produce a 'brick bond'. The tiles are much smaller than typical single-lap tiles, historically 6½in wide by 10½in long – a size standardized in

Fig 40   Extra-wide slates and tiles are needed at valleys and hips to allow firm fixing: otherwise, small pieces come adrift, as here.

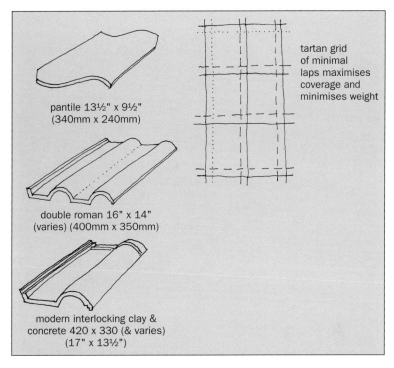

Fig 41   Single-lap tiling – pantiles, double-romans and interlocking tiles.

pantile 13½" x 9½"
(340mm x 240mm)

double roman 16" x 14"
(varies) (400mm x 350mm)

modern interlocking clay &
concrete 420 x 330 (& varies)
(17" x 13½")

tartan grid
of minimal
laps maximises
coverage and
minimises weight

Fig 42   Triple-roman Bridgewater clay tiles.

England in the reign of King Edward IV – and now metricated at 165mm by 265mm, often with a slight camber across the width.

The extra layer of tiles makes double-lap tiling much heavier (around 65kg/m² for clay and 70kg/m².

for concrete) but damage or even loss of a tile still leaves the roof relatively well-protected. Minimum pitches for traditional plain tiles are 35 degrees for machine-made and 40 degrees for hand-made; whereas clay double roman tiles can be laid to

Fig 43   Interlocking concrete tiles centre and right, with concrete plain tiles at left.

30 degrees and modern clay pantiles down to 22.5 degrees. The more sophisticated head- and side-lap details of some modern profiled concrete tiles, allow pitches as low as 12 degrees.

In practice, one of the commonest reasons for rain penetration of tiled roofs is too shallow a pitch for the tiles used. In severe cases, the tiles tend to accumulate moss growth and often fail through frost damage; lesser cases may appear satisfactory until driving rain or snow demonstrates the weakness.

Traditional clay pantiles were often crudely made and poorly fitted. They were usually intended for farm buildings, where plentiful ventilation was seen as a virtue, rather than houses. I have spent many cold

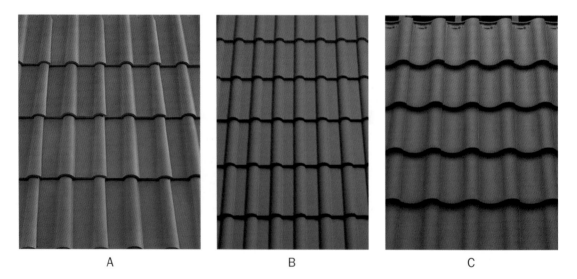

| A | B | C |

Fig 44   Sandtoft's new 'Bridgewater' clay double-roman ([A]left), grey concrete double-roman ([B]centre), pantile ([C]right).

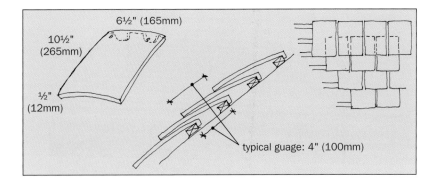

Fig 45 Double-lap plain tiles.

6½" (165mm)

10½" (265mm)

½" (12mm)

typical guage: 4" (100mm)

hours after a powder snowstorm, carefully shovelling snow off the lath and plaster ceilings of a pantiled house without sarking felt. Looking into the loft of a house with no sarking and poorly fitting pantiles seldom needs a torch, since there is so much daylight!

Slates

Slates are laid as double-lap tiles with two thicknesses of slate and three at the head laps. Stone slates, particular in certain areas such as the Isle of Purbeck, the Cotswolds, Cornwall, Westmoreland and parts of Yorkshire and Scotland, are generally laid in a similar way but, to make best economic use of the varying sizes available, they are often laid in diminishing courses, with the largest slates at the eaves and the smallest at the ridge.

Selecting and adjusting stone slates to produce a tightly laid roof requires great skill, as does the quarrying, splitting and finishing of the stone itself. This high labour content made most natural stone slating increasingly expensive during the twentieth century. Even Welsh, Cornish and Westmoreland slates, with their natural propensity to split cleanly and evenly, gradually became high-cost materials, heavily undercut in price by artificial substitutes and imported natural slates from Spain, South America and even China, though a thriving trade in second-hand natural slate has maintained some availability at reasonable cost in this country.

Defects in slate and tile roofs leading to damp penetration can be divided into 'component failures' and 'system failures'.

Fig 46 Clay plain tiles to the right, and a modern lightweight single lap version to the left: note the difference in size and coverage.

Fig 47   Clay pantiles tiles laid at too low a pitch attract moss growth and frost damage as well as serious leakage.

Fig 48   Stone slates laid to 'diminishing courses'.

Component Failures

Component failures are defects in the tiles or slates themselves, usually caused by decay from age or physical damage, most often from weather but occasionally from impacts by debris from higher parts of the building or its neighbours, or from nearby trees, or even from careless maintenance. Component failures are often easy to see, particularly when, for example, a cracked slate comes adrift from its nail fixings and slides down the roof, or when clay tile surfaces visibly disintegrate due to frost damage. With some tiles, and often with slates, the surface covered by the slate or tile above deteriorates faster than the part fully exposed to weather. In checking the condition of slates and tiles stripped from a roof to assess their fitness for re-use, apart from obvious cracks or delamination, it is possible to check 'structural soundness' by tapping them with a metal tool – usually the slater's hook or hammer used for removing them – a sound slate or tile should make a sharp sound with a slight 'ring' to it, whereas a duff one will make a dull, soft sound and should be discarded. Even though the cost of second-hand replacements is high, it is a false economy to re-cover a roof using defective slates or tiles, since they will inevitably fail within a few years and require expensive individual replacement.

Remedying the problem is straightforward if re-roofing is required because the number or frequency of failures has reached a point where individual repair is no longer economic. Since labour costs are now a high proportion of most kinds of re-roofing, it makes sound sense to ensure that specification and detailing are carried out to high standards, for the longest possible life. British Standard BS 5534 2003 is a good benchmark for all traditional roofing workmanship and there are both building text books and DIY manuals on the subject. The opportunity should be taken to replace any mortar fillets at chimneys, copings or abutments with the appropriate lead flashings – the Lead Sheet Association has a good manual of details.

Also fundamental to good roofing practice is an appropriate underlay or 'sarking', since this provides the long-term back-up to the slates or tiles, protecting the building both against the severest driving rain or snow that may penetrate all but the tightest of roofs, and against damp penetration caused by individual slate or tile loss or damage. If there is any prospect of some or all of the roof-space being used for accommodation – and therefore thermally insulated at rafter level – it is advisable to use a vapour-permeable or 'breathable' sarking, as opposed to the traditional reinforced bitumen 'slaters felt' (*see* Chapter 4 for an explanation of this).

More relevant to this book is the appropriate remedying of individual or partial component failure, such as replacing a slipped tile or slate. To an even greater extent than with full re-roofing, labour is the dominant cost of repairs, especially if a slate has simply slipped but not broken. Corrosion of nails is a widespread cause of increasing slippage in slate roofs. Slating nails began to be widely galvanized in the twentieth century and the use of stainless steel or alloy nails is now recommended for even longer life. When corrosion of nails is prevalent, it is often referred to as 'nail sickness' and re-slating or re-tiling is the only effective long-term remedy.

Adhesive Systems   Some roofers and specialist firms have marketed adhesive fixed pads glued to the underside of slates as a way of avoiding wholesale re-slating. The validity of this method depends on the life-expectancy of the adhesive and the quality of

preparation: if both are good and the savings are substantial, then the advantages of sarking, re-battening and a thorough job, may be worth forgoing. This method can at least provide an invisible repair to isolated slate slippages in historic buildings, where the insides of the roof pitches are accessible and the appearance of hooks is not acceptable. The same process can also be carried out using polyurethane foam adhesives applied in small blobs to the inside of individual slates or tiles, but workmanship is even more critical.

What is much less acceptable is the wholesale application of spray foams to the underside of slated and tiled roofs. This treatment is often marketed as a multi-purpose solution to failing roofs, combining the permanent adhesion of the roofing with insulation and secondary waterproofing. While there is no doubt that thoroughly applied polyurethane foam will bond all slates, battens and flashings together, and will provide a slight degree of insulation to a roof-space – 25mm (1in) of polyurethane is equivalent to approximately 40mm of mineral wool insulation quilt, though its performance does deteriorate slowly – it has to be considered what the long-term effects of this 'glue mat' will be on the condition of the roof timbers and how the eventual process of re-roofing may be affected. The build-up of battens and rafters means that the tops of the rafters will not be covered in foam, certainly where crossed by battens, and seldom elsewhere either; this means that any moisture penetrating the tiles or slates tends to collect on, and soak into, the battens and rafters with much less chance of drying-out owing to the foam 'underblanket'. In these cases, the battens are often in a poor state already and their progressive decay can be much accelerated by the foam application. Although their function has been superseded by the foam, their decay is likely to spread into the rafters and other roof structures; such decay can progress unnoticed owing to the foam lining until structural collapse may occur.

A secondary disadvantage of such methods is the loss of the slates and tiles as a re-usable resource, which applies even more conspicuously to exterior coating systems that bond and waterproof the roof with a clear or coloured plastic coating. Such processes have been effectively applied to corrugated

Fig 49   Lead 'tingles' unfolded on a south roof pitch allow slates to slip again.

sheet materials, such as steel and asbestos cement on industrial buildings, where the *in situ* upgrade can be carried out without disrupting production below and extend the life of such roofs by a decade or more.

What may be proclaimed as an advantage of this kind of repair, namely draught-sealing the roof, may actually cause or increase a condensation problem, which can again lead to timber decay and visible dampness, unless sufficient measures are taken to allow for new ventilation of the roof-space (*see* Chapter 4). It is therefore not recommended to use these treatments, either foams or coatings, except as a short-term improvement to a roof – and probably roof structure – that is due to be scrapped.

Tingles and Hooks   It is clear that stable, long-term repair solutions are required: the fact that so many slates are reinstated using lead strip 'tingles', which tend to 'unfold' after a few hot summers – especially on a south pitch, suggests that the roof repairers who fit them are either strangely ignorant or keen to provide themselves with future work. Copper-strip tingles tend to last longer than lead but weather to a conspicuous green. The replacement of an individual slate on a generally nailed roof should be carried out using a stainless steel hook; for standard slating, these are available off the peg from roofing suppliers in

Fig 50   Black stainless steel slate hooks: the best fixing method for individual slate replacement.

black-coated stainless steel; for special slates, they can be simply made by a competent roofer using heavy gauge stainless steel wire bent to suit each slate. In either case, the result is a reliable repair, almost invisible from the ground and likely to last as long as the roof itself. Full re-slating can be carried out using these hooks instead of nails for a longer life. The hook system has the advantages of avoiding both the labour cost and the inherent weakness of holing the slates for the nails, and of securing the slates in a flexible manner, while restraining their bottom edges against wind uplift. There is a subtle 'texture' to a hook-fixed roof, which may not be acceptable to some listed building officers, so owners of listed houses should make discreet enquiries first before embarking on full re-roofing using hooks.

Individual Tile Replacement The replacement of individual tiles is more straightforward since tiles are secured by their nibs and, for most areas of a tiled roof, an individual missing or damaged tile can be replaced by easing adjacent tiles apart and sliding the new tile into the gap until its nibs engage on the tiling batten. The difficulty comes in replacing tiles close to the ridge, hip, verge or valley, where the tiles have been mortar-bedded or nailed so that they are rigidly secured, often preventing the removal of the damaged

tile and the insertion of its replacement: in such cases, it may be necessary to remove several tiles or to 'approach' the replacement from an area of unbedded or un-nailed tiles. Similarly, replacement of individual ridge, hip or valley tiles can prove difficult because of remnants of mortar bedding, although it is often the loss of adhesion in old mortar that has allowed the problem to occur in the first place, which may then make it easier to remove.

Bedding Mortar and Dry Fixing The question of whether to use bedding mortar or 'dry fixing' in these locations is a difficult one: there is no entirely correct answer. The arguments for dry detailing are for speed, accuracy and longevity. Dry-fix components are typically made both from tiling material (e.g. clay, concrete) and from uPVC incorporating ultra-violet stabilizers to protect them against sunlight; they have the advantage of allowing limited movement but their actual life-expectancy is not yet clearly shown to exceed mortar bedding. The dry-fix clay or concrete components – ridge, verge and hip tiles – typically have a plastic base frame into which they are fixed to eliminate mortar.

Mortar bedding has clear advantages in the re-use of traditional roofing tiles, ridges, etc., which will not usually match the current dry-fix fittings. In

Fig 51   Slipping a replacement tile into place to be held by its nibs.

Fig 52   Dry-fix roofing fittings: concrete verge tiles.

Fig 53   PVC verges over a full PVC barge board fascia and soffit installation.

Scandinavia, tile bedding is done using non-setting 'putties', which can better accommodate movement but they have not been successfully marketed in the UK. If concrete tiles are being bedded, it makes sense to use the normal hard 1(cement):3(sand) mortar, but for clay tiles, and certainly for stone tiles and ridges, it is preferable to use a 1(*hydraulic* lime):3(sand) mortar, which will be more flexible and is more likely

to permit re-use of the tiles again when the mortar eventually gives way.

It is also unlikely to be acceptable to use visible plastic roofing components on the roof of a Listed house, though in some cases traditional lead detailing may be an acceptable 'dry-fix' option. For mortar bedding, it may be appropriate to colour the bedding mortar to tone in with the colour of slates or tiles,

Fig 54 Asbestos-cement verge fittings over a metal-clad house that has been refinished with an acrylic textured coating.

Fig 55 PVC verge fittings used to close the gap between new concrete tiles and old asbestos-cement sheets. The house to the left has had its steel cladding replaced with a brick slip facing while the house to the right has had its steel cladding acrylic-coated.

typically black to go with ordinary slates and red-brown to suit tiles.

Large areas of mortar bedding, particularly in the 'pans' of pantiles or other profiled tiles below the ridge tiles, can be prone to dropping out; the traditional detail in response to this is to bed in some 'tile slips' to reduce the bulk of the mortar and make it less liable to shrinkage and loss of adhesion.

System Failures

System failures are due to inadequacies of detail design, workmanship or materials. The most common in older houses are at the edges and penetrations of roofs, where mortar fillets were used as a cheaper substitute for lead flashings and inevitably shrink, crack and frequently break away. Where fillets remain in place, loss of adhesion – particularly to slates – can allow moisture to penetrate unnoticed and lead to timber decay, especially at abutments or chimney stacks, where adjacent masonry can act as a reservoir, soaking up moisture during rain and then gradually releasing it into the adjacent roof timbers, so increasing the likelihood of rot. Even where flashings have been used, failures are still quite common due to poor workmanship, storm damage or corrosion, particularly with zinc.

The importance of sarking as a back-up to tiles and slates cannot be over emphasized and this is probably

Fig 56   Mortar fillets at roof edges crack and break away or simply let in water unseen.

the most important improvement incorporated in re-roofing, particularly now that vapour-permeable sarkings can offer a condensation-free alternative to traditional bitumen felts.

Sarkings   Before the use of bitumen-felt sarkings, better quality roofs, particularly from the Victorian period and later, were often boarded above the rafters, which improved the structural stability of the roof and provided some degree of secondary weather protection, especially against snow, but provided no significant waterproofing against leaks. Earlier than this, some roofs were 'parged' with straw and lime plaster, or lath and plaster, between the rafters, particularly where attics were used for storage or accommodation. Both measures reduced airflow through the roof structure

Fig 57   Tiling at too low a pitch (Fig 56) means saturated and rotting boarding below.

and roof-space, which was clearly an advantage if the attic was inhabited but is not so good for the long-term health of the roof timbers and battens. If roofs are not well-maintained, such absorbent underlayers can become a breeding ground for wet rot, once tiles or slates have slipped and there is insufficient air movement to allow rapid drying-out.

If boarding or parging is to be retained when a roof is recovered, perhaps in a Listed building or for structural reasons, it is important that vapour-permeable sarking is laid above it and that tiling battens are raised above the surface on counter-battens fixed directly above and in line with the rafters. Only in this way can a clear drainage path for any moisture penetrating the tiles be maintained clear of the battens and away at the eaves. The vapour-permeable sarking will allow any residual moisture from earlier leaks to dry out and reduce the possibility of condensation wetting the boarding.

Sheathing   It is seldom necessary to install boarding or 'sheathing' over a traditional pitched roof unless there is a structural need to brace the roof structure – in which case engineers' or builders' advice to install plywood sheathing should be resisted unless absolutely necessary. Plywoods, due to their glue layers, are seriously vapour-proof and so should rarely be installed on the cold outside of roof structures, where they may cause condensation, particularly if any part of the roof-space is used for living space. The one circumstance where plywood sheathing to the outside of a roof structure may be acceptable is when the structure is to be fully exposed internally – in the case of a

visually appealing traditional roof, perhaps. In this case, the roof will be insulated *above* the plywood using high-performance insulation with the counter-battens secured by extra-long fixings through the insulation to the rafters. In this detail, the ply is acting as a vapour check in the correct position – on the warm side of the insulation.

If structural sheathing is necessary in more conventional situations, there are vapour-permeable but moisture-resistant fibre-boards such as Bitvent and Panelvent, which can provide sufficient racking strength in most cases; where these may not be available, square-edge softwood boarding, sometimes laid diagonally and screw-fixed, if necessary, can be used.

The other situation where sheathing may be appropriate is where for historic, aesthetic or perhaps economic reasons, a shallow pitched roof has to be covered with slates or tiles that are not effectively weatherproof at that pitch, in which case the sarking has to work as an effective roof membrane rather than just as an occasional back-up, and so should be fully supported. I was faced with just such a challenge a few years ago at the Yorkshire Sculpture Park, where historic outbuildings had been built with lean-to roofs against a long, curved garden wall on rising ground. To keep below the top of the garden wall, the Victorian builders had constructed the slate roofs at a 14-degree pitch, at a sideways slope to follow the ground, all to a curved plan. This meant that the slates had no chance of being fully waterproof. Frequent leaks over an estate workshop and cart sheds were doubtless tolerated but the buildings had been converted to gallery use in the 1990s and, despite

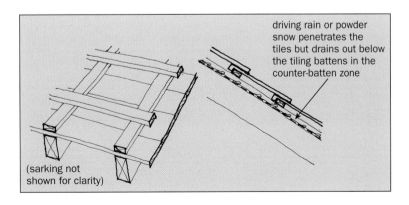

Fig 58   Counter-battens over boarding or taut sarking.

driving rain or powder snow penetrates the tiles but drains out below the tiling battens in the counter-batten zone

(sarking not shown for clarity)

Fig 59   Very shallow pitch slating, curved and...

sarking felt, still leaked regularly and needed a more effective solution.

To allow for the curved plan and sideways pitch, the roof was sheathed in narrow, green larch boards, flexible enough to curve in three dimensions. It was then covered with two layers of vapour-permeable sarking laid radially down the roof and lapped sideways to suit the sideways gradient. Counter-battens were laid to a skewed radial pattern following the combined pitch and sideways fall, screwed into the larch boards and to the rafters, where they coincided. Green larch slating battens again followed the 3D curve.

In cases like this, the slates or tiles provide a visual finish and mechanical and ultra-violet protection to the sarking but it is the sarking that provides reliable waterproofing. Only in such exceptional cases is it worth the complexity and cost of effective roofing below the recommended pitches for slates or tiles as listed in the table.

Roof-Space Ventilation and Permeable Sarkings   In the majority of cases, pitched roofs over an uninhabited roof-space are sarked directly over the rafters and the sarking is laid loose enough to sag between each pair of rafters, so as to allow clear drainage of water below the battens.

If traditional reinforced bitumen felt sarking is used, such roof-spaces can be ventilated via the eaves, the ridge and vents in gables or in the roof-slope itself, but in re-roofing, the cost of such ventilation details is likely to outweigh the extra cost of using a vapour-permeable sarking, which in most cases will make additional vents unnecessary.

Fig 60   ...sloping in two directions, needs elaborate sarking to stay dry.

Typical Minimum Recommended Pitches (in degrees) for Roofing Materials	
Thatch	50
Handmade plain tiles	40
Machine-made plain tiles	35
Clay pantiles	35
Clay double-romans	30
Concrete single-lap tiles	22½
Interlocking clay pantiles	22½
Natural slates (500 × 250mm Countess)	22½
Natural slates (600 × 300mm Duchess)	17½
Artificial interlocking slates	15
Cedar/oak/chestnut shingles	14
Interlocking concrete tiles	12½
Profiled metal-sheet roofing	4
Standing seam-metal roofing	3
Single-ply membranes and felt	2

In the case of an existing roof already felted with impermeable felt, the Building Regulations (Part F2) provide clear advice as to how much ventilation is required for different roof pitches, and builders' merchants or roofing component manufacturers will advise on the fittings needed.

If there is any possibility that the roof-space might be used for accommodation, and therefore need to be insulated in line with the rafters, it is advisable in re-roofing to use a vapour-permeable sarking laid taut over the rafters with counter-battens, to achieve the clearance under the tiling battens. Re-roofing using counter-battens will raise the surface of the slates or tiles by the thickness of the counter-battens – usually 25mm (1in) but can be 19mm ($\frac{3}{4}$in – which can cause difficulties where the roof is laid between gable walls with tightly fitted copings. Sometimes it is appropriate to relay the copings over DPCs, which can accommodate the extra height,

Fig 61   Traditional bitumen sarking felt laid to sag between rafters to drain water below the battens.

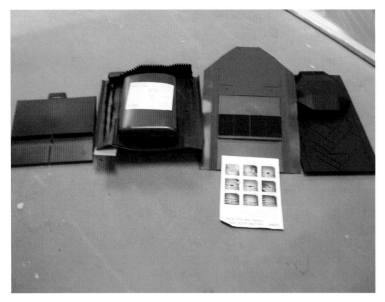

Fig 62   Roof-ventilation fittings for vent pipes, extract fans or simply to vent a roof-space: (left) for plain tiles and profiled tiles; (right) for slates.

but for historic buildings such details need careful consideration.

If insulating between rafters under an existing bitumen felt sarking, a minimum 50mm (2in) air gap has to be maintained between insulation and felt for effective airflow to clear water vapour and condensation. For loft conversions with limited headroom, this can be a significant disadvantage, as well as reducing the capacity for insulation.

Sarkings to pitched roofs in the UK are traditionally laid horizontally lapped by 150mm (6in), though tautly laid sarkings can be laid down the slope parallel with the rafters, which allows the laps to occur over rafters continuously supported.

Bitumen sarkings are laid loose at the laps and their relative stiffness and weight means they tend to remain static, even in high winds; because permeable sarkings are much thinner, lighter and more flexible, there is a risk that they can undulate or flap in high winds, especially when laid to sag between rafters, and particularly at the eaves where they are most exposed. Such movement can be noisy and irritating, and in serious cases can lead to fatigue in the material. This is another reason why taut installation under counter-battens is recommended for permeable sarkings.

In aiming to reduce heat loss through roofs, it has been shown that sealing the laps of permeable sarkings with tape significantly reduces air movement and draughts in the roof-space, while water vapour passes through harmlessly. Although taping the laps of draped sarking is possible, it is much simpler when laid taut: a further advantage of this layout.

Finally, it is important to note the double layer of sarking applied at hips and valleys to back up the necessary joints at these changes of pitch; in each case a separate length of sarking is laid down the hip or valley. At valleys the separate length is laid *under* the normal sarking and at hips it is laid *over* it.

Flashings The traditional good-quality flashing material in the UK is sheet lead, of varying thicknesses – usually Code 4 or 5 (1.8 or 2.24mm). Lead's advantages of malleability, durability and weldability make it hard to equal, although its environmental credentials are poor due to its toxicity, mitigated a little

by its widespread recycling. No effective plastic substitute has been developed and the commonly available Flashband – an adhesive sandwich of bitumen and aluminium foil – provides at best a short-life substitute. Other metals are used, particularly copper and less often stainless steel and aluminium; all are more difficult to work *in situ* by hand, making them more expensive to use and less readily available than lead. Zinc used to be widely used but has a relatively short life, especially in polluted atmospheres, and is now rarely specified except in alloys with titanium, for example.

The principle of using malleable metal flashings in conjunction with roofing components is to allow for waterproofing the changes of pitch and direction at junctions with walls, chimneys, rooflights and other roofplanes. Flashings that are entirely integrated with – and protected by – the roof material, such as soakers and saddles, tend to be the most reliable, hence Code 3 lead (1.32mm) is often specified for soakers. Failures, other than in the material itself, tend to occur where flashings are more exposed to the weather; as, for example, in cover flashings peeled back or dislodged by wind. Their junctions with masonry are also a weakness: the traditional detail is for lead to be folded back on itself and then wedged into a mortar joint with folded lead strip wedges, the rest of the joint then being pointed up with mortar. Owing to movement in the lead and poor adhesion, the mortar pointing tends to work loose and drop out, which in turn allows movement and metal fatigue to progressively loosen the wedges. Some

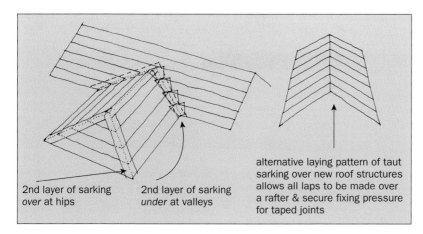

2nd layer of sarking over at hips

2nd layer of sarking *under* at valleys

alternative laying pattern of taut sarking over new roof structures allows all laps to be made over a rafter & secure fixing pressure for taped joints

Fig 63   Roof sarking: double layers at hips and valleys for thorough protection.

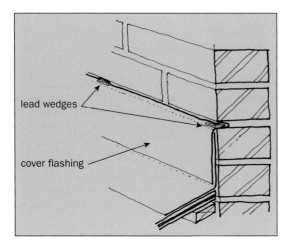

Fig 64   *Lead-cover flashings secured in mortar joints or chases by lead wedges.*

specifications now substitute silicon mastic for mortar pointing but the very flexibility of the silicon that keeps it in place also means that under wind loads the lead can compress the sealant and work loose, so there is no over-riding advantage.

Well-executed flashings are usually reliable for decades and far exceed the life-expectancy of mortar fillets; unlike fillets, flashings can be expected to remain waterproof as long as they remain in place. If water penetration occurs despite flashings still in place, it is likely to be due to poor workmanship or incorrect detailing, or possibly corrosion – especially in zinc – which can occur in the concealed part of the flashing earlier than on the surface. Although it seems like common sense, it is surprising how often laps are made incorrectly, for example, at roof junctions with parapet walls or cavity trays, leading rainwater *under* the roof flashing instead of out and over it.

Where roofs have been added, for extensions or conservatories perhaps, the proper cavity tray detail is laborious and therefore expensive to install. In more sheltered situations, householders or their builders may have decided to take the risk and do without, which may prove satisfactory for most weather conditions – but perhaps not all. For solid walls, the equivalent detail relies on a simple chase into the masonry: if the exposure is too great, the masonry too porous or the chase too shallow, water may soak in beyond the flashing and so penetrate the interior. We will explore remedies for wall penetration later in this chapter.

CHIMNEYS, ROOFLIGHTS, DORMERS AND VENTS

Wherever a roof has an object built into it that interrupts the simple lapped coverings of slates and tiles, it becomes vulnerable to water penetration.

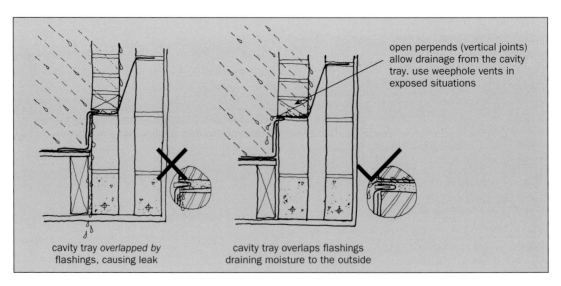

Fig 65   *The crucial detail for cavity trays.*

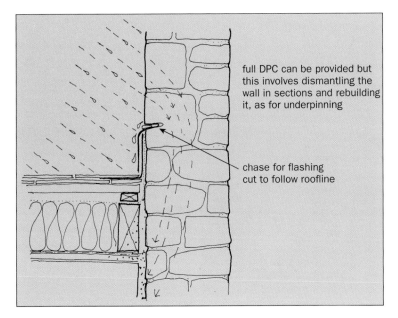

full DPC can be provided but this involves dismantling the wall in sections and rebuilding it, as for underpinning

chase for flashing cut to follow roofline

Fig 66   Flashings chased into solid masonry, overcome by strong driving rain.

Chimney Stacks

The chimney is the classic example of this since its very function of allowing smoke out provides an entry point for rain through the flue – unless this is capped in some way. Flues to open fires tend to have fully open chimney pots and rely on updraught and frequent use of the fires (as they were designed) to prevent a build-up of damp in the stack. Traditional good design of chimneys incorporates a slight bend somewhere in the flue to avoid rainfall directly onto the fireplace, but this rain still ends up inside the chimney. In many houses once totally reliant on open fires for heating, there may be just one fireplace left in use or none at all, but the flues and pots remain as a potential entry point for rain.

Assuming the stacks are to remain in place above roof level, the correct procedure is to sweep the flues, fit vented raincaps to the chimney pots and vents to the blocked or blanked-off fireplaces. Hit and miss vent grilles can be used provided they are not kept permanently closed. If venting of the flues is not acceptable, there is no reliable alternative to dismantling the stack to below roof level.

Although it is important to control the airflow and heat loss through chimney stacks generally, and especially with redundant ones, it is also worth considering their environmental benefits in providing secure, stack ventilation in the summer. As global warming continues apace, householders should think carefully as to whether their chimney stacks may not have a positive future after all, although for the most effective cooling, vents into flues need to be positioned at ceiling level where hot air accumulates.

Traditional chimney stacks out of use will absorb driving rain through the sides of the stack, as well as through the pots, and can produce significant damp problems, particularly in upstairs rooms. Good-quality lead flashings to brick or masonry stacks include a lead tray that sheds water just above roof level. However, many stacks have no leadwork and rely on mortar fillets at the roof surface and projecting masonry courses to shed rainwater before it reaches the roof. Even where lead flashings have been added in the course of re-roofing, they are usually chased into the masonry, since fitting a full lead tray requires the reconstruction of the stack, so dampness can still penetrate, especially the taller stacks in more exposed locations.

The combination of long-term deposits of sulphates from burning coal and dampness can produce highly destructive conditions in unlined chimney flues and stacks, causing mortar joints to expand and lose adhesion, requiring stacks to be rebuilt. Since

Fig 67   Fit vented raincaps to disused chimney pots.

Fig 68   Mortar fillets around chimney stacks are often a cause of damp penetration.

chimney stacks are usually more exposed to driving rain on one side than another, one of the symptoms of sulphate damage – especially in brickwork with its large proportion of joints – is the bent or curved stack from the expansion of mortar joints on one side more than the other. On the path to disintegration, masonry becomes more porous and so more vulnerable to driving rain penetration, which in turn accelerates the corrosive effects and the decay.

Rooflights

Although most of us have become familiar with the Velux – the 'Hoover' of the rooflight world – which is renowned for its reliability and successful detailing, there are millions of houses in the UK built before the Velux era, and large numbers of these have rooflights, ranging from the most primitive small panes of glass, or even profiled glass tiles built into attic roofs, to quite elaborate metal-framed, multi-pane rooflights,

Fig 69   Unequal expansion of sulphur-impregnated mortar joints leading to 'bent' chimney stacks.

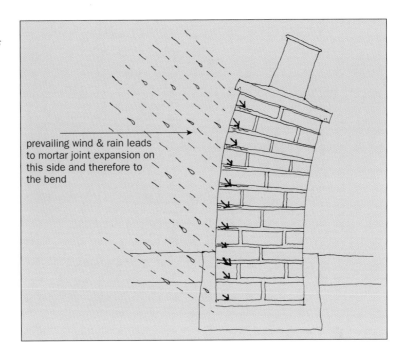

prevailing wind & rain leads to mortar joint expansion on this side and therefore to the bend

including opening lights. In traditional rooflights, moisture penetration tends to occur either through the surrounding flashings – often site-built in a fairly rudimentary way – or through the glazing frame itself and its putty detailing.

For the builder or householder faced with a leaking rooflight, particularly in the context of a general re-roofing, the simplest solution tends to be a full replacement with a modern rooflight, which will often be cheaper as well as offering a huge upgrade in environmental performance and control. However, there are cases, often with historic buildings, where a 'modern rooflight', such as a Velux, is considered unacceptable, which may force owners to either consider the various 'conservation rooflights' – largely metal-framed reproductions of Victorian designs with some modified details to allow for double-glazing and to collect or drain away the condensation on their frames – or to retain and repair the originals. Such traditional glazing can be improved and renovated by the substitution of silicon sealants or neoprene gaskets for the original putties; metal frames worthy of preservation can be shot-blasted or stripped to remove rust and either galvanized or primed and painted.

Just as with other roofing details, the difficulties and cost of access to rooflights make it worth investing in the best possible quality of finishes and details when carrying out repairs. Opening rooflights can make maintenance more feasible, and the typically crude fit of old opening lights will usually allow for the addition of draught-stripping. Replacement of single-glazing with double-glazing can be more difficult, though the use of stepped units, where the outer pane is larger than the inner, so as to retain the same fit in a shallow glazing rebate, can solve this problem (*see* Fig 70).

Apart from glazing seals, the most vulnerable point for leaks tends to be the flashings between the rooflight frame and the surrounding roof: detailing follows the same principles as for any other significant roof penetration with a gutter flashing at the head of the rooflight to drain water to each side flashing, and an apron flashing at the base to discharge water over the slates or tiles. Although for prefabricated rooflights most flashings tend to be pressed aluminium, the aprons for use with profiled tiles, at least and most new site-formed flashings for existing rooflights, will be in lead.

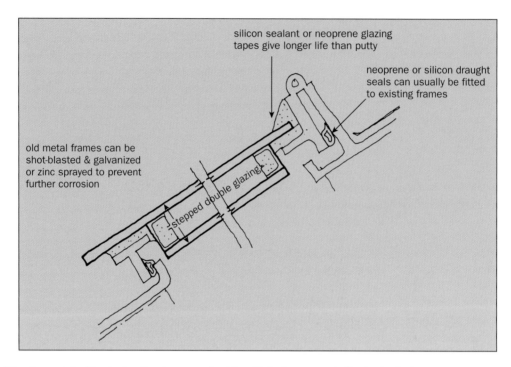

Fig 70   Stepped double-glazing fitted to upgrade old rooflight frames made for single-glazing.

Dormers

Dormer windows usually 'emerge' from roofs in just the same way as rooflights but are more like small buildings perched on the roof rather than mere windows. As such, they have not only the connection zone of the roof flashings to deal with but may also have the full range of wall and roof details of their own, with the added drawbacks of more severe exposure and especially difficult access. Although fully opening window sashes allow for reasonable access to the window itself and its immediate surroundings – particularly if side-hung casements are hung on reflex hinges that allow access to both sides – the side-walls or 'cheeks' of dormers and their roofs, whether gabled, flat or mono-pitched, are seldom safely accessible in this way and so require roof ladders, if not scaffolding. Due to the height and protruding shape of dormers and their high proportion of edge and junction details, they are particularly susceptible to wind and weather damage.

Vents

Most vents through roofs are soil stack ventilation pipes, which need an appropriate collar detail in lead,

other metals, rubber or plastic to underlap tiles above and overlap tiles below. Such collar details in metal often include a soldered or welded joint around the pipe, which may fail through fatigue. Although most vent pipes lead directly into drainage, and so can accept rain entry, some will serve as extract vents from fans or passive stacks, and these need to be effectively cowled to keep out rain. For plastic pipes, cowls or 'mushroom caps' are available, and for metal pipes or ducts, proprietary terminals are available or a clumsier but still leak-proof terminal can be formed with bends.

Major tile and roof accessory manufacturers market vent terminal fittings, both for roof slopes and for ridges, which make for a more discrete finish, particularly using the flush slate fittings or the ridge terminals. Some of these fittings are made to match existing tile profiles, so they can be retro-fitted to existing roofs, as well as incorporated in new work.

Over the last few decades, many domestic roofs, particularly for council and housing association houses, have been peppered with tile vents to improve ventilation to roof-spaces with traditional felt or other impermeable sarking (*see* Fig 72). Although these are has been the combination of a flawed concept and poor-quality materials that has given rise to so many failures, rather than particular villainy in the flat-roofing industry. In fact the term 'flat roof' is generally a misnomer: flat roofs are, or should be, laid to a slight fall so as to drain rainwater away. The lack of adherence to the roofing principles of 'shed and divert' means that any fault in the material or work-manship is almost bound to lead to trouble. The 'flat' surface means that rain is more slowly removed from the roof and any weakness in the roofing material itself, or in its perimeter details and flashings, is likely to lead to leaks.

Traditional flat roofing, until the early twentieth century at least, usually involved metal sheeting, usu-ally lead, and a series of elaborate stepped details and raised joints to keep sheet sizes small enough to limit thermal movement: this in turn meant that flat roofs were expensive, in both materials and work-manship, and kept their numbers down and their quality – generally – up.

Asphalt

Although asphalt – bitumen mixed with sand – was used as construction waterproofing in the Middle East and Pakistan as long ago as 3,000BC, its recent role in waterproofing began in France in the early nineteenth century and it was introduced to the UK by a Mr Claridge after a visit to Paris in 1837. Claridge supplied it to Brunel for various purposes, and asphalt steadily found favour for high-quality waterproofing of masonry and later concrete structures, where its *in situ* application, and limited flexibility, avoided the need for complex joints and steps. Due to the high labour content and cost, asphalt has a fairly small market-share, even in commercial construction, and its use in housing is relatively rare – though it was used for a number of flat-roofed modern movement houses and flats from the 1930s to the 1950s.

The Mastic Asphalt Council [www.masticasphalt-council.co.uk] publishes good advisory literature on detailing and repairs of asphalt roofing. The two most frequent defects in old asphalt roofs are: 'creep' – meaning the very gradual flow of the asphalt at upstands to roof perimeters and steps, which then leads to thinning and eventual fracture of the asphalt at the most exposed top edges; and simple fractures

Fig 71 'Weathering slates' allow vent pipes to emerge through tiles or slates.

likely to be fitted less and less, as permeable sarkings are more widely accepted, there will be a legacy of such vents for decades to come, and a proportion of these will tend to cause leaks either because they were incor-rectly fitted, or because the plastic components eventu-ally fail; less vulnerable but still potentially at risk in severe driving rain conditions are the vented ridge tiles.

Whenever roofs are repaired or overhauled, they should be assessed for opportunities to improve and simplify their weatherproofing. Although historic and traditional roofs may well deserve to retain exist-ing details and features, they may also include more modern alterations and fittings that may no longer be required. For reasons of performance, safety and cost, simpler roofs tend to perform best in the long term.

FLAT ROOFS

Flat roofs are notoriously troublesome, a byword for unreliability and dubious workmanship, but it

Fig 72   Tile and slate vents allow for a more discrete appearance on the roof.

caused by movement in the structure below. In most cases, such defects can be repaired but the work is skilled and needs to be done by competent asphalt roofers.

Bitumen Felt Roofing

The development that caused both the burgeoning and subsequent discrediting of the flat-roofing industry was the manufacture of cheap, bitumen, felt, roof-sheeting, parallel to the growth of bitumen DPCs. The system of felt flat-roofing is commonly known as 'built-up roofing', since it consists of multiple layers of fabric-based bitumen 'felt', usually three, bonded in hot bitumen. Although this composite membrane is very effectively waterproof, its fundamental flaw is its lack of significant flexibility, which in turn leads to stress and cracking in the surface,

particularly where ponding occurs with inadequate falls, and where direct sunshine causes expansion in the felt, or where there is significant movement in the underlying roof structure. Another frequent defect in felt roofs is intermittent blistering caused by expansion of vapour trapped between the deck and the felt or by condensation of internal water vapour. Good-quality installations often include a 'vapour-release layer' and small mushroom-shaped vents to release such vapour before it causes a problem. Without adequate ventilation, the timber decks supporting small flat roofs can decay rapidly due to condensation, which will be discussed in the next chapter.

Standard bitumen felt roofing fully exposed may have as short a life as ten years, which led to the development of 'high-performance felts' by most manufacturers. These substituted artificial fibres, usually polyester, for the hessian backing to basic felts, thereby increasing their flexibility and allowing manufacturers to issue guarantees, typically for a 'twenty-year life'.

The repair of felt flat roofs tends to be an even shorter term prospect than the original roof, unless of course the repair is to physical damage. The reason that repairs offer no long-term reliability is that most flat-roofing defects are integral to the system, rather than a simple matter of component replacement or faulty workmanship. Faulty workmanship will probably cause a felt flat roof to fail and leak sooner but it is less likely to be correctable by repairs, as it often is for pitched roofs.

Short-term repairs to felt-roof defects can include bitumen mastic pointing to cracks, which may last no more than a few months if the problem is underlying movement, or patching over the defect with a layer of more flexible high-performance felt bonded around its perimeter, so as to allow for ongoing movement. We recently specified just such patching to a pitched felt roof over a college building that we were refurbishing for a 'five to ten-year life'. A lack of maintenance had allowed the twenty-year-old roof to develop splits and cracks that had birch saplings growing out of them. However, to renew the whole roof covering with a better material would have taken up far too much of the budget for such a short-life

project, and on a pitched roof, the patches may have a reasonable prospect of lasting for the projected life of the building (*see* Fig 74).

Metal Roofing

Lead
By far the commonest metal roofing on traditional houses in the UK is lead, laid and maintained by large numbers of skilled leadworkers – and, regrettably, also by some less skilled and conscientious. A properly laid lead roof is extremely long-lasting and reliable, and the body of knowledge and craftsmanship, and the literature to back it up, are excellent and widely available. The Lead Sheet Association provides guidance and a very clear technical manual of details and techniques.

Other Metals
Zinc, copper and stainless steel are the competitors for lead, but all are significantly more difficult to work with. Only stainless steel has a longer life and better environmental pedigree than lead but the difficulty of working it, and therefore the much smaller number of craftsmen competent to use it, tends to make it more expensive than lead for small projects. It does have the advantage of a much lower rate of thermal expansion, which means it can be laid in long lengths, so simplifying roof-deck construction, as compared

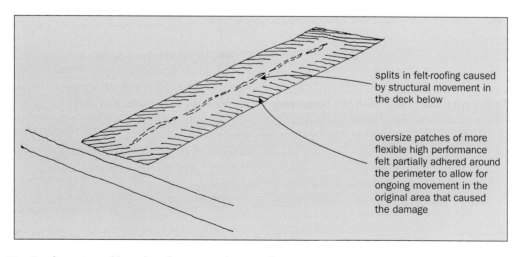

splits in felt-roofing caused by structural movement in the deck below

oversize patches of more flexible high performance felt partially adhered around the perimeter to allow for ongoing movement in the original area that caused the damage

Fig 73 Patch repairs to felt roofs: a short-term solution at best.

*Fig 74   Felt-patch repairs on a
pitched roof for 'a short life
refurbishment of five to ten years'.*

to decks for lead. It is also more resistant to impact damage and vandalism than lead and less liable to be stolen for scrap. Arguably, in its tin-coated form weathering to a soft, pale grey after a few shiny years, it is also a reasonable aesthetic competitor for lead.

Layout and Jointing

Common to all sheet-metal roofing is the trough/upstand arrangement by which trough-shaped lengths of sheet metal are laid down the slope of the roof, side by side; the adjacent upstands of the troughs are then folded or lapped in a waterproof upstand joint detail. For lead, too soft to stand securely on its own, the common detail is to lap the lead upstands around a wooden batten, usually rounded in shape and called a 'roll'. In the stiffer other metals, a thin 'standing seam' detail is more common, unless there is a visual requirement for the batten or roll shape. In good-quality metal roofing, leaks are unlikely, but both poor quality workmanship and the frequently occurring bodged or low-cost substitute repairs to old lead-work are likely to give trouble.

Problems and Repairs

The chief drawback of lead as a sheet roofing is its high thermal expansion, which means that it needs to be laid in relatively short lengths, related to its thickness. The thicker the sheet, the longer the length that

64

Fig 75 A properly laid lead roof is extremely long-lasting and reliable.

Fig 76 Only stainless steel has a longer life and better environmental pedigree than lead: a tin coating allows it to weather to a soft grey after a few years.

can be laid (but the higher the cost). Each sheet junction requires a step for a waterproof detail, usually 50mm (2in) high.

Any movement is most pronounced in full sun; partial sun and shade can increase stress on the lead. Where too long a length or too thin a sheet is used, failure is likely from stress splits or cracks, and although patch or soldered repairs can be done, they will be only temporarily successful if the layout or material is incorrect. If providing the extra step needed to shorten the lead sheet length is not possible, or not economic, neoprene expansion joints formed between two strips of lead can be welded into the centre of the split sheet so as to remove the thermal stress.

Impact damage from vandalism or careless maintenance is usually simpler to repair with solder or a lead patch, soldered or 'lead-burned' in place. If faced with a leaking and previously repaired lead roof or gutter, owners need to get themselves the best advice from a competent lead craftsman, surveyor or architect, since repairs will tend to become more frequent and therefore expensive. Alternatives such as single-ply, GRP, etc. (*see* below), may need to be considered for cost reasons, though in the case of historic buildings, the only permitted alternative to lead may be tin-coated stainless steel and even then, subject to consent.

Metal tiles

In the last few decades, a significant specialist metal-roofing industry has developed to supply simulated rooftiles in larger format, colour-coated, galvanized steel sheets for applying lightweight pitched roofs over flat-roofed buildings. The principal market has been in the refurbishment of local authority and housing association flat-roofed blocks, but the suppliers have diversified into other areas and the same materials have been used on 'mobile homes' and pre-fabricated modular housing, where their closeness to the ground means that they are a less visually convincing substitute for tiles. Although still in their 'infancy' as a roofing material, they are likely to share life-expectancy and repair characteristics with other profiled, colour-coated, metal roof sheets that can either be resurfaced with heavy duty coatings for a short-term extension of their life, or replaced.

Single-Ply Membranes

The most significant improvement in the prospects of flat roofing has been the successful development of 'single-ply roofing membranes'. These are flexible sheet materials that can be reliably jointed by heat or by adhesives to form a complete roof covering. They were developed from the 1950s onwards for large-scale industrial and commercial roofing, and are still most widely used in this sector. A number of different materials are used, including PVCs and various artificial rubbers with lesser environmental impacts, most of which are black, though some are available in greys, brown and green. They can be laid loose and ballasted to hold them down against wind uplift, or mechanically fixed using tabs welded to the underside

of the sheet, or adhered, which tends to be the commonest method.

As long as single-ply roofing membranes are not physically damaged by impacts or careless maintenance work, they have a very long, trouble-free life, seeming to remain unchanged and equally flexible for several decades. Since artificial rubbers (EPDM, etc.) are less environmentally destructive (in both manufacture and disposal) than PVC, and are competitive in cost and life-expectancy, we specify them in preference. The ballasted details have the advantage of providing physical protection to the membrane, so remedying their only significant weakness. The ultimate flat-roofing system uses these membranes in an 'upside-down roof', where the insulation material (waterproof foam boarding) is laid above the waterproofing layer, so protecting it physically, thermally and against sunlight for an effectively permanent solution. There is one type of insulation board with interlocking edge details and a pre-screeded surface that is adequate on its own, but most upside-down roofs need ballast – usually either paving slabs or pebbles – above the insulation to weight it down against wind uplift. The additional weight of this, as well as the deeper roof build-up, means that such solutions may not be appropriate in all cases.

In existing housing, single-ply membranes are particularly appropriate for complex areas of roofing and guttering between other roofs, where there may be insufficient gradient available to allow for the correct series of steps needed for leadwork, or where several penetrations through the roof, perhaps for rooflights and vents, would make leadwork both difficult and costly. We used EPDM – 1mm-thick black artificial rubber – for a small flat roof to a house in Bath over twenty years ago, where the roof area, of only around 5m² (50ft²), included a rooflight and two vent outlets, as well as perimeter upstands all round and an outlet chute in one corner. To fabricate this in lead would have been slow, complicated and costly, whereas the EPDM fabricator worked from my dimensioned drawing and supplied the complete roof sheet, including all the details rolled up as a parcel and delivered to my office. I was then able to carry the bundle onto the roof and unroll it to fit in around an hour; I have been back to check the state of it recently

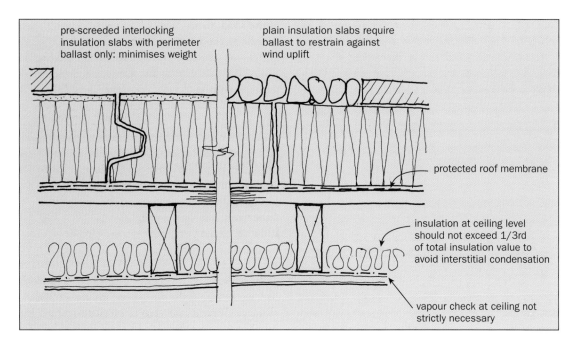

pre-screeded interlocking insulation slabs with perimeter ballast only: minimises weight

plain insulation slabs require ballast to restrain against wind uplift

protected roof membrane

insulation at ceiling level should not exceed 1/3rd of total insulation value to avoid interstitial condensation

vapour check at ceiling not strictly necessary

Fig 77   Upside-down roofs – membrane protected by insulation for a permanent solution.

and the EPDM remains as soft and flexible as the day I laid it.

In situ Solutions

There are two other kinds of twentieth-century roofing material that may be particularly appropriate to repair or replace small flat roofs to houses: one of these is fibreglass or GRP (glass-reinforced plastic), and the second is a patent type of very thin, mesh-reinforced concrete or 'ferro-cement' called Roofkrete. The widespread type of GRP is basically a thinner form of the material used for building small boats, and is very similar to the resin-repair systems used to repair car bodies. Matting of glass fibres is embedded and covered with epoxy resin to build up a very strong and slightly flexible sheet, which is formed *in situ* and so can follow all the intricacies and convolutions of the most complex gutters, upstands and penetrating ducts, vents or rooflights. The work is carried out by specialist contractors and will typically cost less than equivalent leadwork, as well as requiring a less complex timber decking below. Life expectancy is long (though not in comparison to good leadwork), particularly

where shaded from direct sunlight – probably thirty years or more. Other types of liquid plastic coatings are used in a similar way, often with polyester fabric reinforcement, again by specialist contractors.

Roofkrete is an *in situ* system similar in process to GRP but using several layers of fine steel mesh (instead of glass-fibre matting) stapled to timber decking, and a patent cementitious mix trowelled into the mesh, which produces a 6–8mm-thick waterproof and damage-resistant finish that is recommended for balconies, walkways and roof gardens, as well as ordinary flat roofs. Although the long-term performance – and especially corrosion resistance – of this system is somewhat mysterious, it has been used by the original contractors in Devon for over thirty years and is now more widely marketed with a guarantee of twenty years.

Something that all flat-roof coverings have in common is their high degree of vapour resistance, which means that all 'cold flat-roofing' details, where the insulation is at ceiling level, have to allow for cross-ventilation so that vapour can be removed in order to avoid condensation. This and ways to achieve it, as well as alternative approaches, will be considered in Chapter 4.

DAMP-PENETRATING WALLS

Although walls, in both their materials and their details, are even more diverse than roofs, as far as damp penetration is concerned, they can be usefully divided into three categories: solid masonry walls, cavity masonry walls and clad walls. The last category, cladding, also sometimes applies to the other types as we shall see and there can be confusion when masonry, stone or brickwork is used as cladding but designed to appear as 'traditional cavity walling', as has been widely done in commercial and social housebuilding in the UK.

Symptoms

The critical difference in symptoms for penetrating as opposed to rising damp in walls is that the often similar surface effects – damp patches, mould, peeling paint, decaying plaster and timber – occur not just at the lower parts of the wall but high up as well. They may well appear worse at lower levels, either because they are combined with those of rising damp or simply because the amount of rain reaching the base of the wall externally is greater than the amount further up. It is also very unlikely that penetrating damp to walls – from whatever cause – will occur evenly in all walls: if it is due to driving rain, it is likely to be worst in the west or south-west, though local differences in shelter and wind patterns may affect this; if it is due to some specific defect, such as leaking gutters or downpipes, it will also be localized.

Although penetrating damp will usually show itself in association with rainfall, and most often with heavy, wind-driven rainfall, the time-lag for the damp to penetrate thick walls can be considerable, so the link may be a seasonal one rather than observable on a daily basis. On the other hand, if a damp problem in walls were to worsen during a period of sustained dry weather, it would be more sensible to search for leaking services than for rain penetration.

If the symptoms are both evenly distributed and apparently independent of rainfall, they may be due to condensation, which is considered in the next chapter.

Solid Masonry Walls

The way these walls resist penetrating damp is generally by a mixture of shedding, absorbing and evaporation. A typical brick or stone wall will absorb moisture from light rain blown against its surface. As the rain's intensity increases, the surface zone of porous masonry becomes saturated and the water is shed, streaming down the face of the wall and soaking into the ground or running away across paving. Once the rain stops, the porous surface releases the absorbed moisture by evaporation and gradually dries out. Only in extreme and prolonged periods of wind-driven rain will a sound solid wall be 'overcome' and allow dampness to penetrate to the interior. The critical factors are:

- wall thickness – generally the thicker the wall, the longer it will resist damp penetration.
- surface condition – both porosity and especially joints between bricks or stones, and at openings, sills and copings;
- exposure of the wall, both in terms of orientation and local shelter;
- duration: the BRE has surveyed rainfall duration as only 5 per cent of the time in London but as much as 10 per cent in the hilly areas of Wales and the West, and up to 15 per cent in NW Scotland.

Wall Thickness

It is unusual for houses to be built with solid walls too thin to resist penetrating damp. In areas of generally low exposure, such as large cities and particularly London and the south-east, a 'single brick wall', meaning 225mm (9in), i.e. a brick 'header' laid across the wall, was expected to be sufficiently damp-resistant, and provided the wall is well built of sound bricks and the pointing is maintained in good condition, this will be so. In a few areas, Georgian Bath being a classic example, the availability of a readily worked building stone allowed builders to construct housing with external walls as thin as 150mm (6in) and occasionally 100mm (4in), which are remarkably effective at resisting damp, though thin walls in better-quality housing are often lined internally with timber framing finished in lath and plaster.

Although thicker brick walls – 'one and a half brick walls' (338mm/13in) and occasionally even thicker – are used for structural reasons, such as for the lower stories of tall houses or for retaining walls in basements, most thicker stone walls are built as two 'skins' using the best stone for the outer skin, lesser stone for the inner, with occasional stones stretching between the inner and outer skins to bond them together but with the cores generally filled up as construction proceeds with the offcuts, scraps and mortar. The quality of such walls varies enormously, not just in the visible 'face work' but also in the core, Where the core material is of poor quality and the mortar very weak, these central parts of masonry walls often crumble and subside between the inner and outer skin, depositing a loose fill material in the lower part of the wall and leaving irregular voids above. If such walls are exposed to severe weather, penetrating rain can effectively wash weak core materials away with the accumulation of damp material in the core at the base increasing the likelihood of both penetrating damp and rising damp at low level. On the other hand, where the inner and outer skins are well built and sufficiently maintained, the wall can remain stable in the long term and the cavity effect may actually reduce penetrating damp in the upper parts of the wall.

Surface Condition

The porosity of masonry materials, both bricks and stones, varies considerably from the most impervious granites and slates and well-fired engineering bricks, to the weakest and most absorbent limestones and soft under-fired bricks. Although the quality of bricks is largely controlled in the choice of clays and the firing, defective bricks do occur and there are many cases where bricks of insufficient facing quality have been used to reduce construction costs. Although such bricks may perform satisfactorily in many cases, they may be vulnerable to locally increased exposure or to particularly severe frosts.

The absorbency of both brick and stone can change over time and while the more durable surface of facing bricks is formed in the firing, many stones, particularly limestones and even chalk, develop a seasoned face through atmospheric exposure, as illustrated in the BRE's testing of Totternhoe stone in Bedfordshire, where very soft chalky limestone, as quarried, develops an effectively weather-resistant surface over time to allow its use in building. Careless cleaning or alteration work can damage these mature surfaces, increasing vulnerability to penetrating damp and frost damage.

Where the porosity of stone or brickwork has become a problem and the pointing is sound, there

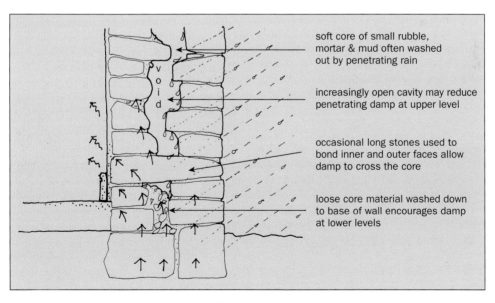

soft core of small rubble, mortar & mud often washed out by penetrating rain

increasingly open cavity may reduce penetrating damp at upper level

occasional long stones used to bond inner and outer faces allow damp to cross the core

loose core material washed down to base of wall encourages damp at lower levels

Fig 78   Penetrating damp in double-skinned, rubble, masonry walls.

are generally three options: clad the wall externally, line the wall internally or reduce the wall's porosity. Cladding and lining solutions are discussed below but reducing the wall's porosity sounds like an attractive option and there is a large range of paints and coatings available to do this.

Paints and Coatings

Assuming that changing the wall's external appearance is not acceptable, spraying the wall with colourless water-repellents, usually silicon or silane-based, is a fairly simple measure, but these treatments have a limited life, often no more than five years or so, which can make them more expensive than other measures in the long term, particularly for taller facades where safe access may require scaffolding.

Although some water-repellents appear to be harmless to most brickwork and sandstones, there has been concern, particularly amongst conservationists, about their effect on limestones; some are certainly not appropriate. Apart from the frequent application of lime-shelter coats, there is no approved solution for reducing water penetration of limestone that does not significantly change its appearance. Before using waterproofing treatments on historic walling, it is wise to seek advice from local authority conservation officers.

Painting walls, and occasionally even roofs, to reduce damp penetration is a very traditional approach.

Stone, brick, earth and concrete walls are all frequently painted to improve their weather-resistance, as well as to upgrade their appearance. Limewash is the original exterior paint: soluble, short-lived and reliant on frequent, and therefore labour-intensive, application. Its popularity dwindled as more complex paint manufacture offered longer lasting, stronger coloured and fade-resistant products, initially using vegetable oil and animal fat binders and later mineral oils with increasingly sophisticated chemical constituents. The advantage of painting to reduce damp penetration is in providing a smoother, water-shedding surface that decreases absorbency, which is pure advantage as long as the paint film remains unbroken and as long as there is no internal moisture needing to evaporate from the wall. However, conventional paints share some disadvantages with strong cement renders in that breaks in the paint film – inevitable over most materials – do allow moisture to penetrate, while the paint film's vapour-resistance has drastically reduced the evaporation rate. Where conventional external paints are applied to traditional walls without damp courses, the problem can be compounded by the effects of rising damp. In many cases, the paint film's adhesion to the wall breaks down under the pressure of water vapour within the wall. The classic symptoms, so often seen on masonry shopfronts, of peeling and flaking paintwork are usually at their worst at low level, where penetrating damp and rising

Fig 79   Silicon-sprayed brickwork shedding water. (Peter Cox)

damp combine in an unholy alliance. Paint manufacturers developed specific masonry paints, both smooth and textured, with household names, such as sandtex, snowcem and weathershield, that gradually improved adhesion, flexibility and permeability, so as to reduce these failures and improve durability.

Painting house exteriors involves serious and costly access problems, which make increasing durability essential; just as the rising cost of labour makes the cost of the paint steadily less significant than the labour cost of its application, and therefore its lifetime before redecoration.

Although the majority of exterior masonry paints were based on oil binders, alkyds and, later on, vinyls, a small sector of the industry in Europe developed mineral paints that worked as a more integrated coating, combining with rendered or masonry surfaces rather than forming a surface film, and retaining much greater vapour permeability. Keim is the best known of these firms [www.keimpaints.co.uk] and

Fig 80   Damp-induced failure of conventional paints on low-level masonry.

claims a lifespan of around double that of conventional masonry paints.

In recent years, there has been a revival of interest in limewash as the 'breathable' exterior treatment for masonry and renders, particularly applicable to limestone walls and to lime renders, where the limewash can have a restorative effect on the surface structure of the stone or render, reinstating lime lost through the long-term effects of rainfall and pollution, while allowing moisture to evaporate freely. However, in terms of reducing damp penetration, limewash still has its traditional disadvantages of solubility and a relatively short life before requiring reapplication. So, if a coating is essential for cement-rendered or cement-mortared brick walls, particularly with difficult access and thereby high labour costs, a longer life is advisable, such as can be offered by one of the mineral paints or the latest, most vapour-permeable masonry paints.

An important caveat for already painted walls is that the existing paint may not be vapour-permeable and, just like an over-strong cement render, may be exacerbating damp problems by preventing evaporation. If the existing finish appears to be a gloss paint, this is very likely to be a problem and it may well be necessary to remove the existing paint before applying the new.

In the case of easily accessible traditional masonry, especially limestone that has been painted, whitewashed or limewashed in the past, it may therefore, still be more appropriate to apply a limewash than a modern masonry paint. Once again, removal of any modern finishes first is likely to be necessary for the new limewash to both adhere properly and to achieve permeability for damp to evaporate from the wall. Limewashes are now available from a number of conservation suppliers and via the internet.

Jointing and Pointing
The most common defect in the damp resistance and general condition of masonry walls, however, is in their jointing and pointing, rather than in the stones or bricks themselves. The critical issue with pointing is that it should be *weaker* than the masonry it surrounds, which also applies to the mortars with which walls are constructed, though not to quite such a degree. Although the temptation may be to apply

strong mortars to repair or make good a wall, this often causes serious damage and is always a waste of cement and therefore of money.

There are two major reasons why the mortar for pointing should be weaker than the walling material. The first is that all walls move very slightly through thermal expansion and contraction, and particularly in the case of traditional walling over traditional foundations, through ground movement in response to changes in moisture levels. The 'stronger', i.e. richer in cement, the mortar is, the more rigid it is and the less it can accommodate movement: this means that the walling material itself will often crack to accommodate thermal expansion or ground movement, whereas a weak mortar, particularly one containing lime, is more flexible and therefore more likely to accommodate the movement. If the movement is severe, the cracks are more likely to occur in the pointing, where they can be easily repaired, than in the bricks or stone. For the most flexibility, pure lime putty or hydraulic lime mortars can be used without cement but these are significantly more expensive than cement mortars, so are most often used in conservation work or with the softer, natural stones. These types of lime – as opposed to hydrated lime, which serves only as an additive in cement mortars to increase their plasticity and flexibility – have the added environmental advantage over cement that they gradually reabsorb most of the carbon dioxide given off during the manufacture of the lime, whereas cement manufacture is a serious contributor to the world's carbon dioxide pollution problem.

The second major reason for using weak mortar is that cement mortars shrink as they set and the more cement they contain, the more they shrink. Strong cement pointing tends to shrink away from the bricks or stones, leaving cracks around them, which water can penetrate.

Less critical reasons include: the reduced porosity of strong mortars, which tends to increase the surface saturation of the walling material, whereas a weaker mortar will 'absorb its share' and so reduce the penetration of the brick or stone; and the permanence of adhesion of strong mortars, which makes subsequent repointing or eventual re-use of the materials difficult if not impossible. For softer walling stones and bricks subject to gradual surface erosion, there is a specific

and vital reason to avoid strong mortars: as the wall's surface is eroded, it needs its pointing to be eroded just as fast – if the pointing is harder and more resistant to erosion, it will be left proud of the masonry's surface to trap rainwater and often cause serious frost damage. This leads to the other significant aspect of pointing that affects damp penetration: the profile. Although there an infinite variety of pointing profiles according to the skills and preferences of the builders, they fall into three categories: recessed, flush and proud. As can be guessed from the warning about surface erosion above, pointing to a profile proud of the masonry surface – most frequently in the form of 'strap pointing' – is not recommended.

Recessed pointing is usually done to emphasize the individual forms or the horizontal coursing of the stones or bricks, which it achieves partly by isolating the masonry surface from its surrounding mortar and partly by the shadow effect it achieves. Although

Fig 81   Strong mortar-pointing left proud of eroding masonry, exacerbates decay by trapping moisture leading to frost damage.

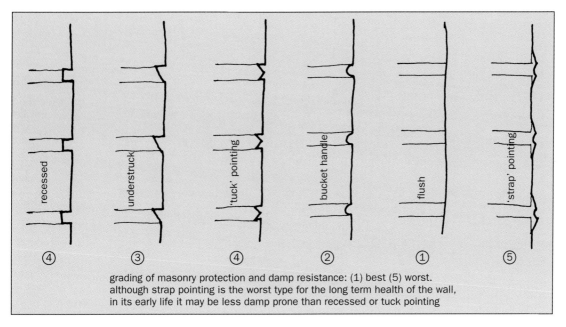

recessed   understruck   'tuck' pointing   bucket handle   flush   'strap' pointing

④   ③   ④   ②   ①   ⑤

grading of masonry protection and damp resistance: (1) best (5) worst.
although strap pointing is the worst type for the long term health of the wall,
in its early life it may be less damp prone than recessed or tuck pointing

Fig 82   Pointing styles.

Fig 83   'Strap pointing' puts masonry walls at risk of frost damage and decay.

recessed pointing can be satisfactory in sheltered situations, it does increase the water penetration of the walls surface. A less problematic detail is 'weather-struck pointing', where the recess is to the underside of the brick or stone only. However, the most efficient way of pointing a wall to minimize water penetration is flush pointing, which encourages the even flow of rain down the wall and the most consistent absorbency across the surface. Flush pointing is finished either truly flush, flat with the brick or stone surface, or to a 'bucket handle' profile, so-called because the original tool for achieving it was a scrap bucket handle straightened out; comfortably handled tools are now widely available to achieve the profile.

Joints at Openings
Every opening in a wall, whether it is for a door, a window, for flues, vents or merely for pipes or wiring, is a potential weakness open to exploitation from penetrating moisture. Better quality masonry detailing – both modern and traditional – at doors and windows includes an overlap of external masonry past the door or window frame. The aesthetic advantage of concealing part of the frame and 'balancing' the exposure of frame all round, is seen at its best in fine Georgian sash windows, but the advantage in

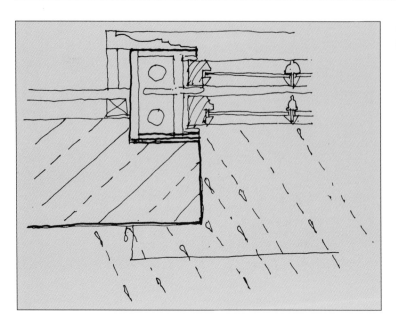

Fig 84   Joinery protection by masonry overlap.

Fig 85   The elegant sightlines of slim Georgian window frames are achieved by sheltering the frames partly behind the stonework.

damp prevention is the blocking of the direct line between inside and outside. Mortar as a filler in these locations is seldom worthwhile because the joinery materials, whether timber, metal or plastics, tend to move at a different rate from the masonry, causing cracks where the two materials join.

The current convention is to use gun-applied sealants – usually silicon mastics – between the dissimilar materials. It is particularly important that the sealant is applied in a bead of sufficient thickness, often 5 or 6mm, so as to allow scope for its movement: the minimally applied triangle of sealant smeared over the surface of a tight joint has little chance. Backing strips of foam plastic or similar can be used to limit the depth of sealant in a deep joint.

Exposure and Duration

Severe exposure of walls is one of the most difficult problems to remedy. The BRE suggests that, although most of the UK suffers wind-driven rain, largely from the south-west and west, parts of the east coast receive wind-driven rain mainly form the north. Exposure can be dealt with – or off-set at least – by any of the methods described in this chapter for improving a wall's weather-resistance, such as repointing, cladding, rendering, sealing joints and so on, but it can also sometimes be dealt with more remotely and

Fig 86   Application of sealant between different materials.

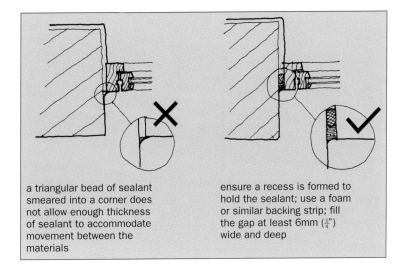

a triangular bead of sealant smeared into a corner does not allow enough thickness of sealant to accommodate movement between the materials

ensure a recess is formed to hold the sealant; use a foam or similar backing strip; fill the gap at least 6mm ($\frac{1}{4}$") wide and deep

less expensively by controlling or influencing the local micro-climate. This is not usually possible for boundary walls but where a house plot includes sufficient space on the windward side, it may be feasible to use trees or other planting – at a safe distance from the wall for its foundations – to divert rain bearing winds away from the affected wall.

Although this might be considered a form of cladding, it is also possible to create a very locally sheltered micro-climate with climbing plants. Evergreen climbers in particular can significantly reduce the amount of rain reaching the wall surface, as well as forming a slightly insulating 'blanket' of air-trapping foliage, which increases the actual wall temperature in winter and decreases it in summer. Care needs to be taken in selecting climbing plants for this role to ensure that they do not damage masonry surfaces. Generally, clinging species such as

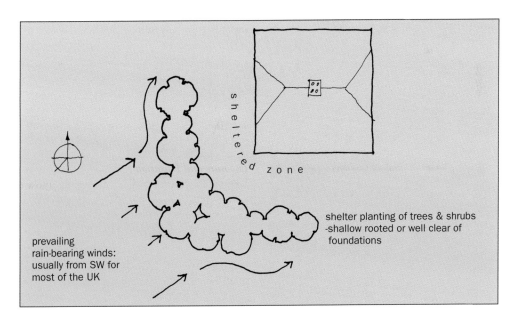

sheltered zone

shelter planting of trees & shrubs -shallow rooted or well clear of foundations

prevailing rain-bearing winds: usually from SW for most of the UK

Fig 87   External protection of buildings by shelter planting.

Fig 88   Evergreen climbers forming a sheltering microclimate against the wall.

ivy and Virginia creeper are risky, whereas twining species such as honeysuckle and wisteria are not. There are sophisticated – and expensive – systems of stainless steel cabling, struts, spacers and tensioners designed for independent support of climbing plants against facades for the 'greening' of buildings, which can serve as micro-climatic protection.

Severe exposure puts most conventional 'water-resistant' construction detailing to the test. A typical standard detail for shedding rainwater from the underside of sills and lintels is a groove or 'throating', and for many standard precast components, these grooves are approximately 10mm ($\frac{3}{8}$ in) in diameter. In calm conditions, such detailing does serve to shed rainwater clear of the wall or joinery below, but I have watched strong wind-driven rain cross three much deeper grooves between lintels simply by wind transfer, 'leaping' each gap to then overcome the door's draught-stripping and frame sealant.

Although even for short periods, severe driven rain can deliver large quantities of water past a building's conventional defensive details, it is only in the most exposed locations that frequency and duration of such conditions warrants the comprehensive wall treatments of cladding or rendering, which not only change the appearance of a house completely but also commit the owners to an ongoing programme of maintenance. Before considering rendering and

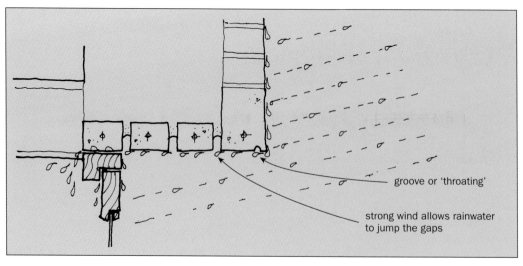

groove or 'throating'

strong wind allows rainwater to jump the gaps

Fig 89   The penetrating power of wind-blown rain overcomes the normal defensive details.

cladding, it is worth assessing the different ways in which cavity masonry suffers damp penetration, as compared to solid walling.

Cavity Masonry Walls

The cavity wall was introduced specifically to prevent damp penetration and is generally very successful at doing so. The principles of cavity walling are that the 'outer leaf', typically 100mm (4in) of brick or stone, or perhaps rendered blockwork, does the primary job of rain-resistance, shedding most of the rain that hits it. However, it is assumed that, in severe conditions, rain will penetrate this outer skin to reach the cavity – originally 50mm (2in) but, now that they are insulated, usually 100mm and often up to 150mm or more – between it and the 'inner leaf', which is some form of blockwork in the great majority of cavity-walled houses. Because the cavity is sheltered from the force of the wind, it amounts to a barrier that the rain, streaming down the inside face of the outer leaf, cannot cross – unless it is 'bridged'.

Cavity Ties

Since each leaf of the wall, usually only 100mm (4in) thick, is structurally inadequate on its own, the two leaves are linked by wall-ties. These are, generally, stiff metal straps or wire ties built into the joints at around 900mm (3ft) centres horizontally and 450mm (18in) centres vertically: such ties would clearly compromise the cavity and allow water to cross it, so they are detailed in various ways to discharge the water before it crosses to the inner leaf.

In early cavity construction, plain steel ties were sometimes used, which inevitably rusted away; even the more general galvanized steel ties have corroded in more exposed conditions, and a significant specialist industry has developed in replacing failed ties with drilled fixings. Although corrosion of ties in itself does not lead to damp penetration, if it spreads from the cavity into the masonry, it can damage the mortar joints and make them vulnerable to damp, so accelerating the rust. The use of stainless steel for ties has virtually overcome the corrosion problem, but the tie remains a weak link in the cavity wall's defence against water penetration, as well as an increasingly

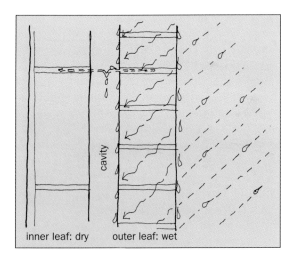

Fig 90   Rain protection by cavity walling: even in strong winds, the cavity is sheltered enough to prevent rain crossing it – as long as there are no 'bridges'.

Fig 91   Typical cavity wall ties are detailed to shed water at the mid-point: the red disk is added to retain partial fill insulation.

significant thermal problem, as cavity insulation reaches higher standards.

Cavity Insulation

In cases of general dampness penetrating cavity walls, it is likely that bridging is occurring consistently, with the most common faults being mortar droppings on wall ties and poorly installed cavity insulation. The most problematic form of cavity insulation, widely installed in the 1970s but now largely discredited, was *in situ* injected plastic foam, with many installations leaving fissures between different patches of setting foam. Since these foams expand into place and adhere strongly to surrounding masonry, they can be very difficult to remove to remedy problems.

The two most widespread retrofit cavity insulation types are now loose polystyrene beads or mineral fibre, both of which can be blown into place (*see* Fig 93). Reputable specialist installers should always insist on carrying out a site survey of existing cavities to check that the cavities are clear and not 'bridged' by faulty cavity ties, mortar droppings or other debris. On the basis of such checks, and good workmanship, some installers will issue a guarantee against damp penetration (of the filled cavity walls) for the life of the building. The wider the cavities are, the less likely they are to suffer damp penetration and the more exposure they can tolerate; for example, with 150mm (6in) fully filled cavities (and flush pointing to external brickwork), a six-storey construction on an exposed estuarine site in NE England was still guaranteed.

The equivalent 'hand-built' details for cavity walls can include prefabricated 'batts' of mineral fibre or slabs of foam insulation board with tongue and groove edges, which are inserted by the masons as they construct the wall. As with most construction materials, in good hands they perform well, although they are less free of risk than dry blown injected systems and are not offered with the same guarantees. The most common defect with site-built full-fill cavity insulation is bridging at the joints through mortar droppings. Both the mineral-fibre batts and the polystyrene slabs rely on a close fit at joints to prevent water tracking across the cavity: mortar droppings on either type can prevent this close fit. A good mason or bricklayer will protect his cavities with a board or will drop little mortar and clean it up scrupulously when he does – but not everyone is so careful.

To avoid such risks, designers and builders sought compromise solutions in cavity masonry, which was partly insulated but retained a cavity outside the insulation: these details used the same sort of mineral-fibre batts or foam-insulation boards but in thinner versions, which are then retained in place by simple plastic clips fitted to the cavity ties, so as to retain an effective clear cavity width. Although some cavity walls were built with the traditional 50mm (2in) cavity partially filled, with, for example, a 25mm (1in) insulation board, good practice requires the full 50mm cavity to minimize the chances of water crossing it. Although the theory of fitting and retaining these partial-fill panels in place is reasonable, the crude and messy reality of most building sites, particularly in bad weather, makes consistently good workmanship difficult to achieve. It only takes a board inaccurately cut or a clip left off to provide an easy route for water penetration (*see* Fig 94). In the early 1980s, I had to check a construction site in Bristol where we had specified partial fill; the number of instances of defective work, even from a reputable contractor, has led me to exclude this detail ever since. Ironically, the same width cavity, fully filled, produces a better insulated building, usually at lower cost and with a guarantee available.

An alternative approach to partial-cavity insulation, which retains most of the cavity width open but split in two parts, is to suspend a foil and plastic composite sheet at the centre of the wall ties, again retained by clips, and lapped with adjacent sheets both horizontally and vertically. These products usually consist of two layers of aluminium foil separated by one or two layers of polythene 'bubble wrap' and encapsulated by further clear polythene to protect the reflective quality of the aluminium. Although in good hands the detail is effective and reliable, the insulation achieved is no better than 25mm of foam-insulation board and good workmanship is at least as difficult. More sophisticated multi-layer foil/foam composites are available but their cost is very high and, according to the BRE, their manufacturers' performance claims are often wildly exaggerated by more than three times the actual value.

Although there is little evidence so far of well-fitted cavity insulation contributing to damp penetration,

Fig 92   Blown mineral-fibre cavity wall insulation: 150mm (6in) wide cavities fully filled and guaranteed against damp penetration, even for a six-storey coastal construction. (Martine Hamilton Knight Photography)

the very fact of its increased complexity makes the chances of defective workmanship greater and, in the case of either foam-injected insulants or partial-fill insulation, the remedying of defective details can be extremely difficult.

Cavity Wall DPCs

The details of cavity walls that protect the integrity of the cavity against water penetration, particularly at openings with vertical DPCs, horizontal DPCs at sills and cavity trays at lintels or 'heads' above the openings, are all potential weak points, since the cavity is 'bridged' in each case and requires the DPC or tray to close the bridge and prevent moisture reaching the inner leaf of the wall. Every junction between the different kinds of DPCs has to be fitted correctly and,

although the principle is simple – to lap the upper DPC over the lower so as to shed the water towards the outside of the building – it is surprisingly common to find DPCs lapped incorrectly. The one exception to the rule about lapping and shedding water to the outside of the building is in one of the most vulnerable locations, the roof parapet. Here, where a cavity wall rises above a roof and is capped by a coping, the DPC is formed as a tray sloping down towards the inner leaf to emerge above the roof upstand at least 150mm (6in) above the roof surface. If the detail were reversed so as to shed water to the outside of the building, the internal face of the parapet would be left vulnerable, which could then direct moisture down the inner leaf (*see* Fig 95).

A second common source of problems is in the end and junction detailing of sills and cavity trays,

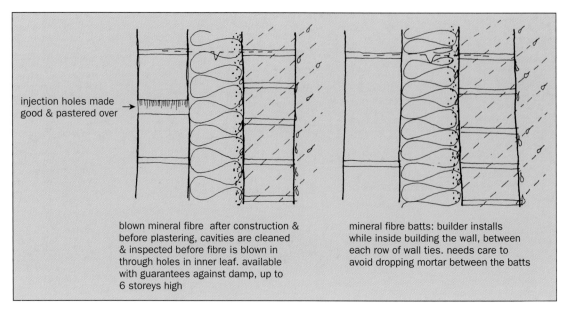

injection holes made good & pastered over →

blown mineral fibre after construction & before plastering, cavities are cleaned & inspected before fibre is blown in through holes in inner leaf. available with guarantees against damp, up to 6 storeys high

mineral fibre batts: builder installs while inside building the wall, between each row of wall ties. needs care to avoid dropping mortar between the batts

Fig 93   Fully filled cavity insulation.

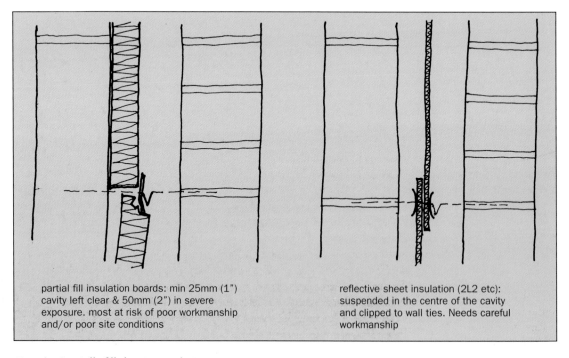

partial fill insulation boards: min 25mm (1") cavity left clear & 50mm (2") in severe exposure. most at risk of poor workmanship and/or poor site conditions

reflective sheet insulation (2L2 etc): suspended in the centre of the cavity and clipped to wall ties. Needs careful workmanship

Fig 94   Partially filled cavity insulation.

Fig 95   Cavity trays at parapet walls.

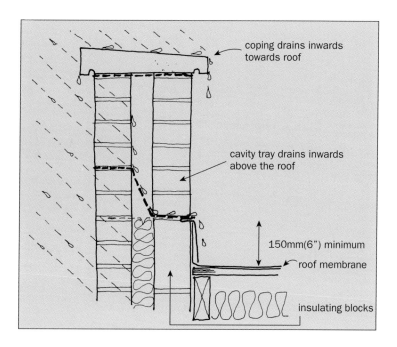

coping drains inwards towards roof

cavity tray drains inwards above the roof

150mm(6") minimum

roof membrane

insulating blocks

where these are subject to prolonged or severe driving rain. Where a cavity wall extends perhaps one or two storeys above an opening for a door or window, or above an abutting roof, a substantial quantity of moisture from rain penetrating the outer leaf can accumulate at the tray. The correct detail at each end of the tray is to form a stop-end within the cavity so that all water is directed outwards through the 'weep holes' above the lintel. Although DPC manufacturers offer 'pre-formed stop-ends', as well as adhesive and instructions for folding and gluing the DPC material to make a stop-end *in situ*, it is not uncommon for the end detailing to be missed out or to be poorly done, which can leave the wall vulnerable to water discharging from the tray ends and reaching the inner leaf. Similarly, for pitched-roof abutments, where stepped cavity trays are used to follow the slope of the roof, the steps should be formed from continuous folded DPC or using pre-formed steps; where each stepped tray is simply overlapped above the tray below (*see* Fig 96). It takes only a moment's careless fitting of the tray at a slight backfall for water to trickle back under the tray and into the internal part of the wall below. In

sheltered situations, or in moderate rainfall, such poor workmanship may go unnoticed. The occasional severe storm, or a change in the degree of exposure due to the felling of a tree or demolition of a nearby building, can therefore produce unexpected signs of penetrating damp around openings or below a roof abutment.

Remedying defects in cavity trays can be particularly difficult due to the need to work in short sections, so as to avoid structural damage to the wall. Such work needs care and experience, as well as a clear understanding of the structural implications. For most situations, reliable and experienced local builders will have the appropriate skills, but the larger problems may well warrant the advice of a building surveyor, architect or structural engineer. Repairing tray ends at each side of an opening is usually simpler because access can be made beyond the bearings of the lintel. For retro-fitting awkward cavity tray details within the grubby confines of a cavity, it may prove simpler to either use the pre-formed tray components available from DPC manufacturers, or to use lead sheet, which can be worked and shaped to deal with the less conventional situations.

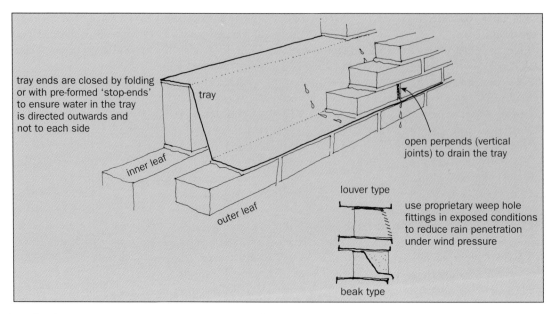

Fig 96   Cavity trays protecting openings in cavity walls.

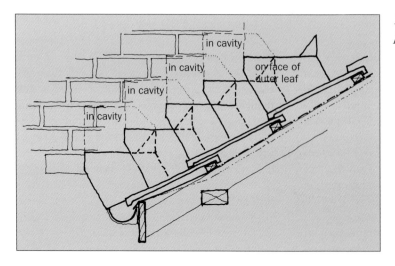

Fig 97   Stepped cavity trays at pitched roof abutment.

Wall Claddings

Although the basic principle of wall cladding is simple – to provide a 'raincoat for the house' – the range of materials and details is bewilderingly large, including timber boarding, slates and 'mathematical tiles', renderings and metal sheets. In short, any material used for roofing can also be applied as a wall cladding, though not necessarily with the same details.

Strictly speaking, masonry materials such as brick and stone, applied as an external, non-structural skin to a building, also count as claddings. While the use of thin panels of stone cladding, restrained by ledges and clips, is widespread in prestigious commercial buildings, this is rare in housing where the widest use of masonry cladding has been in brick skins to timber-frame houses – a hybrid system where the self-supporting outer leaf is restrained by ties back to the timber frame.

From the 1920s to the 1960s, 'system-built houses' employed various claddings of concrete, metal or asbestos-cement panels or tiles over their steel, timber or concrete frames. Although dismissively nick-named 'prefabs', the single-storey, lightweight, timber-framed houses, usually clad in asbestos cement and built during and after both World Wars, have proved enduringly popular. For this book, claddings are relevant both as methods of resisting damp penetrating other walls, and as subject to damp penetration themselves.

'Rainscreen' is a widely used term in commercial cladding and refers to open-detailed, fully ventilated systems, such as timber boarding or metal panels, where there is no close lap or seal in the cladding itself; in contrast to systems such as lapped metal sheeting, boards, slates, tiles or rendering, where the cladding is the primary barrier and may not rely on a back-up sarking or sheathing behind it. This rainscreen is a relatively recent introduction in claddings generally and is therefore rare in houses, at least until the late twentieth century.

The history of cladding as a means to prevent rain penetration is as old as roofing. The most exposed areas of the country, particularly coasts, include numerous examples of slate, tile and timber cladding, often limited to just the most severely exposed facades.

Just as the majority of cladding materials have historically been used as roofing, so their vulnerability to damp penetration is largely covered in the roofing discussion above. However, there are two materials, render and timber, that are not included in these but constitute a substantial part of 'clad houses' in the UK:

Render

Render is the on-site application of a cement or lime-based mix with sand, or other aggregate, to external vertical surfaces – it is the external, and therefore water-resistant, version of plastering. Under this heading are included all texture variations, such as wood float, pebble-dash, harling, spar-dash, and so on. since they are all applied in accordance with the same basic rules and suffer similar problems. Along with the wide range of final textures, there is a significant range of thicknesses from the semi-structural harlings common in Scotland, to the relatively modern,

coloured acrylic decorative coatings that count more as textured paints, at only 1 or 2mm ($\frac{1}{16}$in) thick. BS Code of Practice 5262 provides advice on materials, mixes and workmanship.

There are two main kinds of backgrounds for applying renders: the solid wall to which the render is applied direct, and the framed structure, which supports a 'carrier' of wooden laths, metal lathing or mesh, onto which the render is applied. The same basic rules apply to rendering as to mortar for pointing masonry: that the mix should be no stronger than necessary and certainly no stronger than its background. Strong cement renders have been widely used in the mistaken belief that their high cement content – typically one part cement to three parts sand – produces a more weather-resistant result, whereas the reverse is generally the case.

The three categories of faults with render that lead to damp penetration are: first, cracking; second, debonding; and third, decay. Strictly speaking, debonding needs to be accompanied by cracking to lead to damp problems (it usually is) but since it arises differently, we will look at it separately.

Cracking

Cracking to renders is common and often very visible. It can range from the harmless to the disastrous, though cracking to renders over timber-frame structures is generally more serious than over masonry because of the greater risk of decay. Cracking is usually caused by shrinkage of the render coat itself after application or by movement in the background.

At the harmless end of the scale are scarcely visible hairline shrinkage cracks, uniformly distributed. Providing these occur in a vapour-permeable render of modest strength, they may cause no problems – they may become more or less visible according to weather.

More serious, and usually requiring repair, are less frequent but larger cracks, large enough to allow water penetration at 0.5mm or more, and tending to occur at stress points close to openings, and at floor levels. Where these cracks have appeared soon after rendering, they may be due to shrinkage, and simple repair may be successful. If they appear at likely areas of movement in the background, they will probably reappear after repair, and re-rendering to include movement joints or local reinforcement may be necessary.

Repairing render cracks is difficult to do well, particularly in the smoother finishes, and especially troublesome in unpainted finishes. Where the background can be considered damp-tolerant, such as masonry or brickwork, and if it is known or suspected that the render was carried out with a moderate and vapour-permeable mix – no stronger than one part cement to six parts sand, for example – it may be preferable to leave the cracks unrepaired. However, where damp penetration is a problem and cracked render seems to be a possible cause, the cracks should not be ignored.

Except in the case of historic buildings and an 'original render', removal of the cracked render and re-rendering is likely to be the best course. If this is not possible or not affordable, the best prospects for crack repairs are as follows:

- Rake out the cracks to a minimum of 6mm ($\frac{1}{4}$ in) wide and to the full depth of the render coat(s) that has cracked.
- Remove dust and debris by vacuuming or blowing.
- Either fill the cracks with a gun-applied flexible sealant, such as silicon (or acrylic for a painted finish), where appearance is not critical (for self-coloured, unpainted finishes, a clear sealant may prove less conspicuous than a pigmented one).
- Or, wet the cracks and fill with a slightly weaker mortar mix than the render, using a similar or slightly finer aggregate. For cement or cement–lime–sand renders, the repair mix should include extra-hydrated lime; for example, if the render is thought to be a 1(cement):6(sand) or a 1(cement):1 (hydrated lime):6(sand), the repair mix could be 1(cement):2(hydrated lime):6(sand).

Only sufficient water for the mix to be workable should be added since extra water will increase shrinkage and make recracking more likely. If such crack repairs are carried out to a strong cement render, they will not improve its ability to release moisture by evaporation and, although the repairs should reduce rain penetration, there may be little or no reduction in dampness, especially where rising damp is an additional cause.

If the render is thought to be a traditional lime mix – in which case it will be soft enough to be scratched away with a finger nail – it is essential that only lime putty or hydraulic lime is used for repairs, without cement. In this case, the mix will be much richer, probably 1(lime):3(sand).

Occasionally, a relatively hard hydraulic lime render will be found, which might warrant a 1:2 repair mix but this will depend on the strength of both the original and of the new lime. Advice should be taken from the lime suppliers, from local conservation officers and from builders used to working with traditional limes.

There are several specialist suppliers of cementitious repair compounds for concrete, screeds and renders. For substantial repair jobs, their representatives may be able to visit the site and advise, but most householders are more likely to be relying on their builder, surveyor or architect for advice on small scale repairs. As with most repairs, it is worth trying to establish the cause of render failure before repairing, so as to reduce the chances of re-occurrence.

Two of the principles of successful rendering are that the render mixes should be slightly weaker than the background, and that the render layout should be 'in sympathy' with the building it covers. There is no point in applying continuous, unjointed render to a wall of differing materials and openings because the render will crack along the stress lines. By using appropriately placed movement joints, usually formed by incorporating stainless steel or galvanized metal beads, inevitable movement can be allowed for and both long-term weathering and appearance improved. Weather-sealing these metal-edged joints can be achieved in sheltered situations by simply using a 'belcast' upper bead to overhang the joint or, in more exposed locations and for vertical joints, two metal beads are set 6mm ($\frac{1}{4}$ in) apart and the gap filled with silicon sealant.

For very weak backgrounds, or mixed materials, an alternative approach is to apply metal lathing to the whole wall surface to provide both a consistent key and reinforcement over the junctions between materials. For the conversion of two cob (mud) walled barns in Dorset in the 1970s, where numerous new openings and brickwork repairs to the cob, as well as the irregular rubble-stone base to the walls made a jointed layout impractical, we nailed galvanized expanded metal sheets over all wall surfaces and rendered them with two weak coats of 1:1:8 and 1:1:9 cement:hydrated lime:sand, with the first coat reinforced with chopped

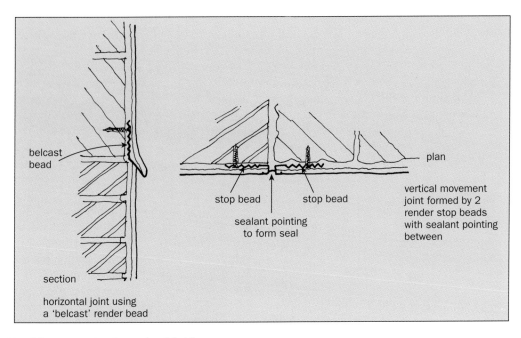

Fig 98 *Movement joints in rendered finishes.*

Fig 99 *Using a 'belcast' metal render bead to overhang and weatherproof the change of materials.*

polypropylene fibre. Thirty years later, the pigmented render remains uncracked and apparently comfortable over its varied background (*see* Fig 100).

Debonding

Debonding of renders from their backgrounds is almost as common as cracking. Fundamentally, it results from an inadequate 'key' in the background, which usually means that the background material is too smooth, perhaps too dense and too impervious for the render mixes applied to it. Traditional masonry materials rely on raked out – or unpointed – mortar joints to provide sufficient physical key for the render to hold. For masonry using large blocks, the joints may be too widely spaced and the stone surface may have been hacked to enhance the key.

Very smooth, dense materials such as engineering brick or concrete require a 'keying coat' or 'spatter-dash', usually of a strong dryish mix spattered onto the masonry and left to set. Since there is no way of retrospectively providing an improved key, debonded rendering nearly always requires replacement. Where the area debonded is relatively small, it may be safe to leave it in place. Larger areas can be secured to their background for safety's sake by mechanical fixings

Fig 100   Thirty years later, the pigmented render remains uncracked over its varied background.

with screws, plugs and washers, but if appearance is important, re-rendering over an improved key will be needed.

Occasionally, historic buildings may need renders restored and re-attached by grouting, but this is specialist conservation work. For most historic buildings, renewal of their detached or damaged renders in appropriate materials is the proper course.

For frame buildings, the key is normally provided by lathing. Traditionally these were narrow, horizontal strips of timber lath nailed to the frame; now widely superseded by various forms of metal lathing, most commonly expanded metal mesh in galvanized or stainless steel. The key to timber laths is provided by setting the laths slightly apart so that the render mix is squeezed between them. Similarly, the gaps in metal lathing allow partial penetration of the render mix.

Debonding can occur when the protruding part of the render cracks off, or when the lathing itself fails through timber decay, rusting nails or corrosion of metal lathing. Traditional render first coats on lathing were reinforced with horse hair or similar natural fibre to improve their key and strength in bonding to the lath; modern renders can be mixed with glass fibre or chopped strands of plastic fibre to achieve a similar and longer lasting effect.

For historic buildings, particularly for the finely decorated 'pargetting' – relief-decorated external plasterwork – widespread in East Anglia, it may be necessary to replace timber laths like for like, but elsewhere the relatively small price differential between stainless steel and galvanized lathing make the stainless steel better value in the long term, given the high labour content in repair or re-rendering.

*Fig 101   Render allows sculptural expression in
following the lines of old buildings – and still
keeps the damp out.*

Render Decay

Render decay occurs for a variety of reasons according
to the mix, the location, exposure and so on. Traditional
lime renders are relatively weak and soft, which makes
them good at accommodating movement and absorbing and releasing moisture, but also makes them eventually vulnerable to erosion and more susceptible to
pollution damage than stronger cement-based renders.

Among the many advantages of traditional renders
is their ability to 'decay gracefully' without causing
damage to their background, due to their permeability. Even when they have been eroded to the point
where moisture penetration of the wall increases, that
moisture will readily evaporate. This contrasts
markedly with strong cement renders, which in failing – usually by a combination of cracking and
debonding – can allow significant rain penetration at
the cracks, which is then prevented from evaporating
by the impervious render, even where this may have

debonded. This leads, in many cases, to completely
unsuccessful efforts to reduce rain penetration of
exposed masonry walls by application of strong
cement renders, which shrink, crack and lead to more
serious problems than those they were meant to solve –
particularly since they can reduce evaporation from
rising as well as penetrating damp, so adding to the
original fault.

Rendering to chimney stacks can suffer from sulphate damage from the flue gases. In severe cases,
re-rendering may be short-lived, even if flues can be
lined, since the salts remain in the masonry and can
still affect the new render. Use of sulphate-resisting
cement will improve the life of cement renders in
these situations.

Improvements to weathering details in capping to
the stack, flaunching around chimney pots and good
overhanging details will reduce rain penetration of
the render and masonry, and should improve the life
of rendered finishes. Wherever possible, rendered
stacks should be avoided, since they tend to be an
ongoing maintenance problem.

Timber Cladding

Traditional timber cladding ranges from the most
open of rustic weatherboarding, equivalent to pantil-
ing in its loose fit and poor resistance to driving rain,
to the tarred boarding of seaside towns that is maintained to be as waterproof as a boat's hull. They each
have their place as traditional claddings but need very
different maintenance and repair.

Board Types

Since timber is worked locally by carpenters, there are
more variations to cladding types than there are to
tiling, but it is still reasonable to identify five common types:

• Wany-edge boarding has its edges left unsawn, as
  they come from the tree, and usually with the bark
  still in place. Originally, it was crude and cheap,
  involving least sawing when sawing was a highly
  laborious and expensive process. Once power saws
  became commonplace, fully sawn timber cladding
  was clearly more economic in its coverage and
  wany-edge boarding only survived as a picturesque
  rustic motif.

- Feather-edge weather boarding is sawn with a diagonal cut and is fixed through the feather-edge under the lap from the board above; this makes for economic coverage and well-protected fixings, while the sawn finish maximizes the life-expectancy of the timber itself.
- Ship-lap boarding is machined – and normally planed smooth to give a more 'sophisticated' appearance than feather-edge – to allow a 'flat overlap' to the board below. Fixings are again protected by the lap of the board above but the planed surface of the boards will tend to require more maintenance than the sawn equivalent. 'Unfinished' planed timber does not last as long as would its sawn equivalent, so ship-lap is generally painted or stained.
- Board and batten is typically used vertically, with the lapped battens fixed to close gaps between the boards. Fixings for the battens at least are exposed but the offset between boards and battens improves air circulation and therefore durability of the timber.
- Rainscreen boarding can be at any angle and has its boards set apart. Although some horizontal boarding is chamfered to divert rainwater to the outside, the shape of the boards is not critical, since the waterproofing is achieved by the sarking membrane behind its supporting battens. For timber rainscreen cladding, the gaps are critical to its long-term success, since they allow for the air circulation that allows the timber to dry out and therefore – in the case of naturally durable timbers at least – to outlast its closely lapped equivalents.

Since effective sarking membranes are a relatively modern arrival in construction, traditional timber cladding has had to do all the work of weather protection and therefore has been closely lapped to keep out both rain and wind.

Coatings, Paints and Stains
Although some traditional timber cladding has been done in oak or, occasionally, in other durable timbers that do not rely on coatings to maintain their integrity and weatherproofing, the majority of surviving cladding dates from the nineteenth or twentieth centuries when cheap softwoods were combined with paints, oils or tar products. While the thinner preservatives, such as creosote and later more sophisticated water- and decay-resistant stains, preserve and waterproof the timber boards individually, the thicker coatings, such as paints and particularly tar coatings, work by producing a wind- and water-resistant film over the whole surface of the cladding.

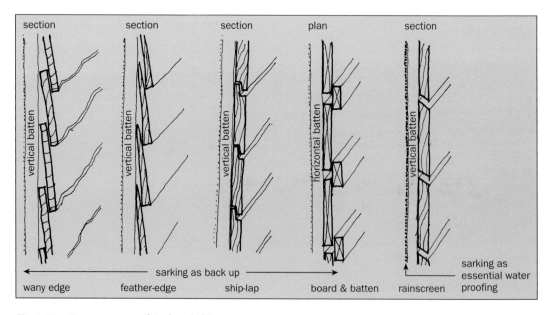

Fig 102 Common types of timber cladding.

Since timber claddings move significantly with changes of temperature and under wind pressure, continuous surface coatings have little chance of staying intact and rely on frequent maintenance to retain their waterproofing; without this, cracks follow the board joints and allow water penetration, which is then retained within the boarding by the waterproof coating and tends to cause decay. Householders with tarred or painted timber cladding may therefore be faced with a choice of either frequent maintenance or of recladding. Unless the cladding is all easily accessible, recladding is likely to be the sensible option, and since the purchase cost of the timber is a relatively low proportion of the overall costs, including fixing and maintenance, it makes sense to select as durable a species as can be afforded, which will either need no treatment or only at long intervals.

Treatment, Sarking, Fixings and Repairs
Similarly, if less durable softwoods are used, these should be pressure- or vacuum-treated to increase their lifespan. Although it is advisable – and now a requirement of building regulations – to install a sarking membrane behind any new timber cladding, to reclad a traditional building with rainscreen timber boarding may not be possible due to its different appearance.

Fig 103   Rainscreen cladding: air gaps allow timber to dry and minimize risk of decay.

Fig 104   Hardwood claddings benefit from movement-tolerant fixings with oversize holes and washers.

89

If a painted finish has to be reproduced, boards should be painted with microporous paints *before* they are fitted, so that the boards are protected all round and have a reasonable prospect of drying-out.

Local repairs of small decayed or damaged areas of timber cladding are always possible; indeed, part of the charm of venerable timber cladding may be its 'visible history' of numerous repairs.

It is worth following the existing cladding in timber species, shape, size for best results, though fixings may be upgraded from nails to screws if needs be, and from iron to galvanized or stainless steel.

Movement stress on boards can be reduced by fixing through oversize holes with washers; although this is more laborious, it is particularly recommended for hardwood boarding, where the harder timber is less accommodating of restrictions to movement at fixing holes.

Verge and Eaves Protection

Applying new timber cladding to upgrade a wall's weatherproofing involves as complete a change in its appearance as rendering or tile or slate hanging. Like tiling and slating, timber cladding means a significant additional thickness to the wall, probably of 40–50mm ($1\frac{1}{2}$–2in), allowing for the supporting battens, which in turn may well need an increased verge or eaves depth to the roof above. Providing an effective roof overhang of at least 50mm (2in) but preferably 100mm (4in) or more, is as important to timber claddings as it is to render.

Corners and Reveals

External corners in timber cladding, traditionally a weak point detailed either as a simple vertical batten or overclad with vertical boards or close mitred, are now more reliable due to the sarking membrane behind. Although clumsier in appearance, the overclad vertical boards give the most reliable result, as they allow for both shrinkage and movement. Similarly, edge details need to be formed at openings for windows and doors, where the frame can project to form a 'stop' for the cladding or be lapped by it; the former detail has the advantage, with horizontal boarding, of protecting the end grain.

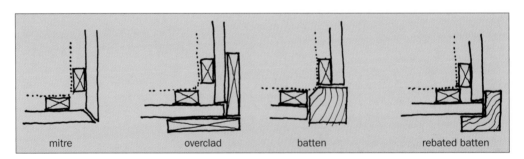

Fig 105   Corners to timber cladding: plan details.

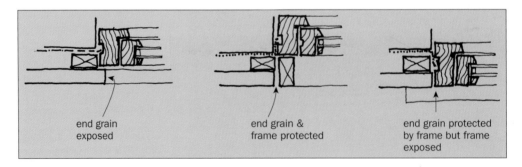

Fig 106   Jamb details at openings in timber cladding.

Tile and Slate Cladding

A widespread traditional cladding of walls against rain penetration uses the same tiles and slates as roofing. Most often seen on weather-exposed gable end walls, where the underlying masonry walls have ceased to – or perhaps never did – keep the interiors dry. Tile – and to a lesser extent slate – hanging is also widely used over timber-frame structures.

Fixing

What makes vertical fixing different from pitched roofing is the greater vertical load and consequent need to nail all tiles, even where they seem securely held by their nibs. In strong winds, it is remarkable how much apparently stable 'surfaces' of tiles and slates will 'ripple': without nailing or traditionally pegging, such winds can strip tiles from a wall despite their nibs. Just as in roofing, the repair, and certainly the recladding, of a tile or slate-hung wall should be taken as an opportunity to incorporate a vapour-permeable sarking beneath new counter-battens and tiling battens. Not only will this significantly improve the severe weather-resistance of the cladding but it

will also allow for evaporation of penetrated or rising damp, where this may have been previously trapped by impervious bitumen felt or polythene sarking.

Mathematical Tiles

Tile hanging for general use occurs widely in Kent, Sussex and E. Hampshire; a variation of this cladding is mathematical tiling (also known as mechanical tiles or brick tiles), which provided a cheap 'visual upgrade' of a timber-framed building to the fashionable appearance of brickwork from the mid-eighteenth to mid-nineteenth centuries. They were not only cheaper to install than a true brick facade but avoided payment of the brick tax. Provided they have not been pointed in cement mortar, the brick tiles can usually be salvaged and re-used (with second-hand to match, if they can be found), if, for example, their supporting battens or framing have decayed. They do form a very effective weather-screen but do not allow for ventilation of supporting timberwork, so are likely to be retained for historical reasons, or where applied over 'lower grade' masonry materials like flint or rubble.

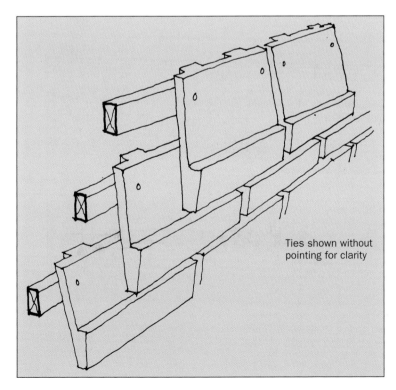

Ties shown without pointing for clarity

Fig 107   Brick-tile cladding – 'mechanical' or 'mathematical' tiles.

DAMP PENETRATING FLOORS AND TANKING

Floors are where it is most difficult to tell penetrating damp from rising damp and where the two kinds of dampness most frequently combine. Suspended floors, whether of traditional timber or of modern concrete construction, are clear of the ground and so, by definition, unlikely to suffer penetrating damp, except in the extremes of flooding. The vulnerability of traditional solid floors to dampness has already been discussed in Chapter 2. Penetrating damp takes the same route into solid floors, often with dramatic results. Since penetrating damp requires the force of gravity or wind pressure to carry the moisture into or onto the floor, the most vulnerable situations are where floors are even slightly below external ground levels. Penetrating damp through walls also often appears most conspicuously at floor level and it may be difficult to define the actual route in detail.

The range of solutions to rising damp in floors already described can be applied to curb penetrating damp. The floor's vulnerability to penetrating damp, both in damp-proofed traditional and in modern solid floors is greatest at the joints in membranes and therefore most commonly at the floor's edges, where the membrane meets the walls.

Tanking

Tanking is the waterproof lining of buildings to keep moisture out: it is applied to critical areas at floor/wall junctions, and to basements and vaults, where whole rooms or storeys are fully below ground.

Ground-Level Tanking

This term is usually applied to substantially below ground waterproofing. The margins to floors between DPMs and DPCs are often referred to simply as 'blacking', tarring, 'RIWing' after one of the current manufacturers, or even 'synthaprufing' after one of the bitumen emulsion tradenames, now defunct. In many houses where surrounding water-tables are low and walls are at least normally water-resistant, the fairly casual attitude of some builders to this marginal detail between floor DPMs and wall DPCs may cause no problems but it can be critical and conditions can change; for example in degrees of exposure, in external ground levels or even in water-table levels.

In modern construction, the floor DPM – usually polythene sheet – is lapped with the wall DPC, which

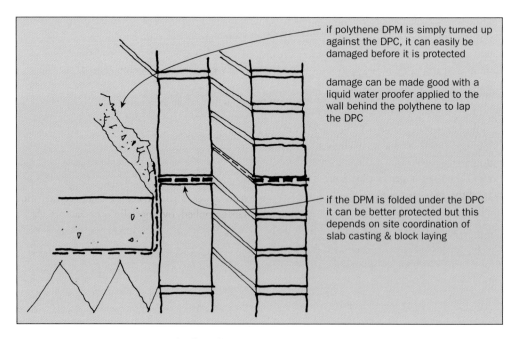

if polythene DPM is simply turned up against the DPC, it can easily be damaged before it is protected

damage can be made good with a liquid water proofer applied to the wall behind the polythene to lap the DPC

if the DPM is folded under the DPC it can be better protected but this depends on site coordination of slab casting & block laying

Fig 108   DPM connection to DPC: risk of site damage.

should be a simple and reliable detail. However, in the rough conditions of most building sites, it is easy for this polythene sheet margin to get damaged before it is adhered to the wall or protected by being tucked into the masonry joint to lap the DPC. Although such damage may be simple to repair with waterproof tape, it can easily go unnoticed.

In traditional solid-wall construction that has had a DPC retro-fitted, by whatever method (*see* Chapter 2), it is very likely that this new DPC will be installed above internal floor levels and that the damp-proof installer's specification will include waterproofing the walls internally below the new DPC. This would typically involve removal of existing plasters and renders, re-rendering with waterproof or at least salt-resistant mixes and then at least two coats of a liquid waterproofer, with the top coat 'blinded' with sharp sand to form a key for new plastering. All these processes require careful and conscientious workmanship to produce a reliable result.

Typical faults in this work are inadequately raked-out masonry joints resulting in an inadequate key for the new render and a reservoir of salt-rich mortar in the joints that can expand and 'blow' the face of the render and plaster finishes. If the new render is poorly finished, it will be difficult to apply the liquid waterproofer completely and small gaps may be left even with two coats. If the render itself is not effectively waterproof, damp will penetrate these imperfections and reach the plaster.

Below-Ground Tanking

The materials and systems used for tanking are varied and subject to gradual evolution as new techniques and products are developed and less successful ones wither away. The main types can be divided into the 'barriers' and the 'diversionaries':

- Barriers include cementitious compounds such as Vandex, liquid polyurethanes, epoxy or bitumen-based waterproofers, mastic asphalt, and sheet DPMs.
- Diversionaries include numerous drained or vented cavity details, both in masonry construction and in void-forming sheet materials, such as Newtonite Lath and Newton 500.

Barrier Types

Barrier materials are effective only by forming a total seal, since they stop the passage of moisture and, in many cases, resist the resulting build-up of water pressure.

Liquids

Water pressure makes barriers susceptible to any defects in either the barrier application or in the surface to which it is applied. For example, in a liquid-membrane application to masonry basement walls, if either the membrane itself is imperfectly applied, or if the masonry background is unreliable – perhaps through minor movement cracks or in its surface damaged by expansion of mineral salts, as described above – the tanking may fail. Many of the plastic and bituminous liquid coatings do have a significant degree of flexibility and may be self-healing over hairline cracks, whereas the cementitious tanking materials, usually sprayed or brush-applied as a thin slurry, are very vulnerable to movement in masonry backgrounds.

Cementitious

Despite appearances of monolithic stability, masonry structures do move and fine movement cracks are common. With traditional lime mortars, such movement is accommodated; but cementitious coatings do not have the same flexibility and tanking failures of these materials due to movement are not covered under installers' guarantees. The false security of such guarantees was well demonstrated in a housing association project where we were converting the stone vaults of small houses to serve as bathrooms. We recommended a diversionary platon system (as described below) to our clients but they insisted on a 'guaranteed system', which meant using cementitious systems applied by specialist contractors. Six houses were treated in two separate contracts, so using separate specialists and tanking products: out of the six houses, four failed within the first year, of which two had to be completely re-treated. The guarantees lasted ten years and even the men doing repairs to the partially failed tankings had no confidence in their work lasting more than a few years before it failed again.

Asphalt

Mastic asphalt has been used as a high-grade tanking material since the nineteenth century and, unlike the cementitious materials, it has sufficient flexibility to withstand significant movement. Its application, trowelled in place as a 12mm ($\frac{1}{2}$ in) thick coating to both floors and walls, is a specialist job at significantly higher cost than most other methods. In tanking, asphalt requires a 'loading screed' above a floor application and lining walls of brick or block to support wall applications, which further increase both its cost and its reliability, as well as taking up space.

Bituminous Screeds

There was a tendency in the 1950s, before polythene membranes dominated the DPM market, for builders to apply various bituminous screeds as waterproof floor finishes. Whereas a correctly applied asphalt provides a reliably waterproof and high-quality floor finish, the weaker versions, with excessive sand content, habitually fail after some years of use, especially if the floor finishes above are disturbed. We found just such a finish applied in a 1950 barn conversion and in the course of researching appropriate remedies, I spoke to a DPM specialist who had worked for a city council in the 1960s and 1970s, and had spent years removing such floors from their

houses. The principal difficulty in this case is cleaning the concrete underneath to remove the bituminous residues so that the new DPM can adhere successfully. Manufacturer's instructions for preparation tend to be very demanding. In the case of the barn conversion, we opted to take up the concrete, which was of poor quality, and start again with a polythene DPM, insulation and a new floor slab.

Epoxies

Whereas most liquid and sheet membranes also require a loading screed to hold them down to the floor against water pressure, some water-based epoxy products have sufficient 'grip' of a clean base material to be applied without a screed and still resist modest water pressure.

Sheet Tankings

The self-adhesive sheet membranes for tanking rely on laps at the edge of each roll of material; since the rolls are usually 1m (39in) or 1.2m (47in) wide, the laps are frequent and workmanship, both in preparation and in installation, is critical. In order for the manufacturer's guarantees to apply, the masonry surface has to be finished to a very high standard, either in fair-faced concrete or in carefully trowelled render. The self-adhesive sheets have to be applied evenly without wrinkles or trapped air, and the lapped joints

Fig 109   Poor-quality bituminous screed from the 1950s.

have to be firmly rolled to achieve a reliable bond. Such good and consistent workmanship is very difficult for builders in the less than perfect conditions of a building site.

Critical Details

Due to water pressure, barrier treatments are also extra vulnerable at all junctions between walls and floors, and where services such as drainage, gas, water and electric supplies enter the building, as they usually do below ground level. Where liquid-applied barriers are applied in stages, either to suit the length of a working day or to allow the building work to proceed (for example, where a floor coating is completed in advance of basement walls), it is necessary to lap the subsequent coating over the first. Even where this lap detail is subsequently 'loaded', perhaps by building a wall or laying a screed over it, the thoroughness and cleanliness of the lap is critical to its success. During construction of a new basement archive store in Bristol, this kind of lapped joint failed, despite advice from the supplier and supervision on site by the client's clerk of works. It is virtually impossible to prove the cause of such a failure because investigation tends to destroy the 'evidence'. It was likely that dirt or debris had built up on the first coat and was not cleaned off before the second coat was applied, allowing water pressure to force its way between the two layers, despite the masonry wall built over it. In this particular case, we had specified a land drain at floor level right around the basement and the contractor was able to install a twin-pump system connected to this drain, which effectively removes the water pressure – as long as the pumps keep running.

All of these problems and potential problems suggest that, for any demanding tanking situation, where walls and floors are significantly below ground, the tanking method should be a diversionary detail rather than a barrier. The one disadvantage that these methods have for a full basement, where there is no lower ground or lower sewer to which water can be drained, is that they rely on pumping to extract the water that is diverted by the tanking. In fact, the British Standard for tanking (BS 8102 1990) specifically recommends a drainage system to back up barrier-tanking

systems, simply because there is always a risk of failure due to poor workmanship, and remedial measures are so difficult. However, in many cases, there are partly lower ground levels, or at least lower drainage levels, that do allow gravity drainage.

Diversionary Types

Diversionary tanking relies on a drained cavity between the wet wall and the inner surface. The size of the cavity is not critical provided it is over 6mm ($\frac{1}{4}$ in) and, where impervious materials are used, it does not even have to be continuous.

Drained Cavities

Traditionally, such a detail is formed by building an inner leaf of masonry set apart from the outer, wet, basement wall with a drainage channel at the bottom of this cavity. This is a reliable, robust and simple solution but it has the disadvantage of occupying significant space: a minimum of 140mm ($5\frac{1}{2}$ in) and usually 175–200mm (7–8in). Although it is possible to form a similar detail with a timber frame inner leaf lined with polythene sheet, successful handling of the polythene sheet is difficult and there is no space gain compared to the more robust and damp-resistant masonry version. However, better insulation can be achieved between timber framing than with insulating lightweight blockwork. Due to the polythene membrane in the cavity, it is essential that the warm side of the insulated studwork has a carefully fitted vapour check, otherwise condensation may occur on the inside face of the cavity membrane and cause decay in the timber framing.

Platon Systems

The most compact way to achieve this cavity drainage detail is to use one of the plastic 'platon' sheets – rather like a tougher version of the lining of a box of chocolates, except that all the chocolates are the same shape! The original material of this sort, Newtonite Lath, is a corrugated sheet of bitumen fibre that was nailed to damp walls and plastered over. Its traditional detail, with open vents at the top and bottom of a wall, was not for wet-tanking but for protection of finishes from damp, since it isolated plaster from the damp surface and allowed air to

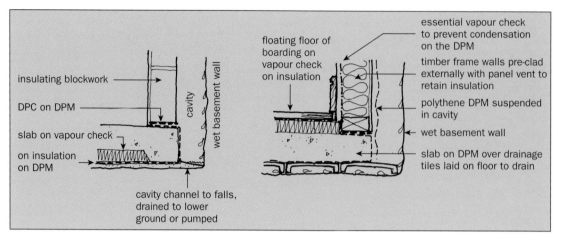

Fig 110   Basement tanking – drained cavity walls.

circulate in the corrugations. Its originator, John Newton, now supply plastic platon sheets for full tanking. These sheets are nailed or screwed to the wet wall, or simply laid over a wet floor, and then either rendered and plastered direct – in which case a platon sheet is used that has a fibre mesh bonded to its inner face to provide key and reinforcement for the render – or dry-lined with plain plasterboard or an insulated laminate of rigid foam and plasterboard. Below floor level, the platon sheets are lapped by the floor DPM and drain to a conventional land drain or to a perimeter sump system if pumping is required.

Although these platon sheets do require closely spaced fixings, usually at 150 or 200mm (6 or 8in) for the direct rendered detail, these fixings are straightforward and subsequent fixing into the wall can be done with no great complication. Typically, for

a plug and screw fixing, the wall is drilled and, before the standard plastic plug is inserted, a small amount of mastic is injected into the hole, then the screw is fixed normally. Because there is no water pressure at the point of penetration, thorough waterproofing is not needed. The reason for this is that, in contrast to the barrier methods of tanking, the platon sheets allow space for water to drain away, so preventing the build-up of water pressure that makes any barrier system vulnerable to imperfect workmanship or to subsequent puncture from fixings.

I first specified one of these materials for the refurbishment of four, very derelict, five-storey terraced houses in central Bath in the 1980s. Three of the five storeys were below street level but open at the rear. Below street level, the front 'wall' of the houses was partly a bare rock face, which streamed with water in wet weather. At the lowest level in two of the houses,

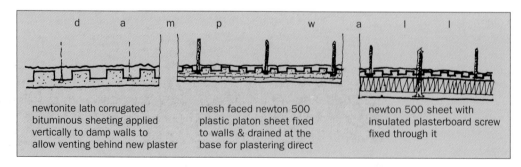

Fig 111   Platon-type tankings – plan details.

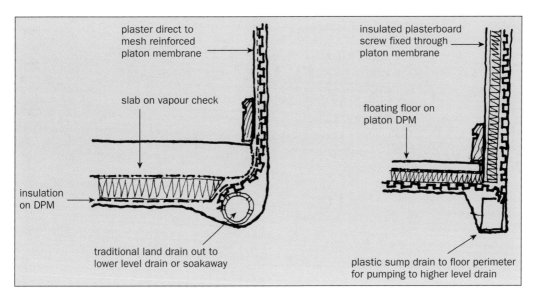

Fig 112   Drainage of platon tankings – section details.

Fig 113   Terraced Georgian houses built into the cliff – two storeys to the uphill side...

Fig 114   ...and five storeys to the downhill side, meant three storeys of platon tanking to the streaming cliff face.

small vaults had been undercut back into this wet rock face. With five party walls and fifteen separate floor structures abutting this wet cliff, it was clear that conventional tanking would have little chance of success. The party walls both support the cliff and achieve their stability from their 'grip' on it, so it was not practical to isolate them. They were conventionally injected, which has proved reasonably successful. The remarkable success has been the platon tanking, which has proved entirely effective for more than twenty years, including at the lowest level, where even the undercut vaults have remained dry. I worked on these buildings again five years ago to alter their accommodation layout: although further damp-proofing was needed in some places for the injected party walls, the platon tanking required no remedial work.

Pre-Finished Tanking to Vaults
Another method of tanking, particularly appropriate for vaults, was developed as a low-cost solution to providing an 'ablutionary' or washing space for the Bath Islamic Centre in the early 1980s. The building has an 8m (26ft) long semi-circular stone vault extending from its basement under the street, which had a further vaulted level below it over a stream running at right angles and parallel with the street above – so drainage was not a problem. A heavy duty single polythene sheet, large enough to line the whole vault, was laid out on the floor. Four long, single 'planks' of standard white plastic weatherboarding were bent into a horseshoe-shape and carried under the sheet and 'sprung' into place at intervals down the vault to support the sheet against the masonry. Due to the shape of the vault, and the natural spring in the plastic planks, no fixings were required. The whole length was then lined with the same planks providing a fully finished, washable and double-waterproofed lining: first, with the plastic sheet and, second, via the planks themselves, which have a self-draining, interlocking edge detail. The uneven stone floor was then covered with a single layer of large, round pebbles to allow free drainage from the edges of the sheet and planks to the central aperture to the vault below. All this was covered with a polythene DPM, concrete slab and tiled finish.

Fig 115   Low-cost tanking and interior finish to a dripping stone vault, lined out this ablutionary below street level.

Although there are certainly success stories for barrier-tanking systems, and there are some full-basement situations where they appear to be necessary due to lack of drainage, my experience has led me to seek diversionary tanking solutions wherever possible, especially where running water is or may be present. Even where a barrier system is adopted, it is advisable to make allowance for secondary drainage and, if necessary, pumping provision to account for the possibility of workmanship defects or building movement.

Finally amongst types of penetrating damp – and most traumatically – there is flooding, but flood protection is a specialist field of engineering and construction that has its own literature, so this book touches on it only with reference to drying-out in Chapter 6.

CHAPTER 4

Condensation

Condensation is the most complex and mysterious form of damp; yet the principle is simple – that warm, moisture-laden air meets a cold surface and the moisture condenses (*see* Fig 4). There are two broad types of condensation problem: interior and interstitial. 'Interior' is the straightforward type visible in interiors; interstitial is less obvious because it occurs between the layers of construction that make up a building's skin.

INTERIOR CONDENSATION

A survey of UK housing in 1986 found that over 20 per cent suffered condensation on windows and nearly 19 per cent had mould or decoration damage. What makes it more difficult to identify and to track is that the occurrence of condensation is subject to so many variables: humidity, ventilation and temperature in the air and permeability, texture and insulation value in the materials. At least the materials stay the same but conditions in the air are so variable over time, especially in Britain's erratic climate, that symptoms range from fleeting through intermittent to seasonal.

Vapour Content of Air

The warmer the air, the more moisture it can hold in the form of vapour, until it becomes saturated and liquid water appears. For example, a given quantity of air at 20°C can hold four times as much moisture as the same quantity of air at 0°C. Humidity is usually measured as relative humidity, which is the actual amount of vapour in air expressed as a percentage of the maximum amount of vapour that air could hold up to saturation. For example, if air, initially at 20°C

with a relative humidity of 70 per cent, is cooled, then condensation will occur at 14.5°C; whereas if this air at 20°C has a relative humidity of only 40 per cent, then condensation will not occur until it is cooled to 6°C. These temperatures, at which condensation occurs, are called 'dewpoints'.

Although the dewpoint must be reached for liquid water to appear, the moulds associated with condensation conditions will grow once the relative humidity has risen to around 80 per cent, equivalent in the two cases above to 18 and 9°C, respectively. Characters of various relative humidities might be described as:

- 90–100 per cent: 'steamy';
- 70–90 per cent: 'humid';
- 50–70 per cent: 'comfortable';
- 30–50 per cent: 'dry';
- below 30 per cent: 'dehydrated';

but the perceived humidity and relative comfort will vary considerably between individuals, as well as with activity levels and air movement. Persistent central heating will often reduce domestic relative humidities to below 50 per cent, leading to the use of humidification or interior planting to maintain reasonably comfortable conditions.

Historical Background

Traditional housing rarely suffered from significant condensation, since internal temperatures were low and ventilation rapid; what heating there was, by open fires or stoves, did raise temperatures locally but in so doing greatly increased ventilation rates. Even in kitchens where steam was generated from cooking, the open hearth fire and large chimney acted as a very effective extract mechanism. It is likely that summer condensation from moist, warmer outside air reaching internal masonry that has retained its low winter temperature, often mistaken for rising damp, would have been a more common problem than the winter kind.

Rising Standards

Over the last century, there has been a series of improvements both to houses and to the ways that people live in them, such as draught reduction, insulation and higher heating standards, which, though understandable and necessary in themselves, have often served to increase levels and frequency of condensation. At the same time, rising living standards have included greatly increased water use and, furthermore, use within houses rather than in yards or gardens, particularly in the areas of personal and clothes washing, and drying. Design and detailing of new houses, and certainly the effective upgrading of old houses, has lagged behind changes in prosperity and behaviour. To make matters worse, many of the early improvements to the housing stock, though effective in their primary objectives, for example of reducing drafts, have resulted in greater condensation and increased the health problems that go with it.

Innocent Condensation

However, it would not be fair to denounce condensation entirely: there always have been and will continue to be 'innocent' or tolerable condensations. Inside millions of cavity walls, internal moisture vapour passes through the relatively warm inner leaf of the wall, crosses the cavity and meets the inner face of the cold outer leaf, where it condenses – interstitially – trickling down the masonry. But this is so similar to the effect of driving rain from outside that there are seldom ill effects, and the condensate drains away harmlessly at the base of the wall or evaporates in the strong air currents that often develop in uninsulated cavities.

A second classic example is the result of the widespread use of bitumen sarking felt as an underlay in re-tiling houses. This is an impervious material installed at the coldest surface of the house over leaky plaster ceilings through which steam from bathrooms

readily migrates. This leads to a dramatic increase in condensation and occasionally to drips and damp patches on ceilings but in most cases, because the traditional roof-space is extremely draughty, even after bitumen felt sarking is fitted, the majority of the condensation is literally blown away and evaporates harmlessly.

Risky Improvements

More serious problems arose when houses were 'further improved' by the addition of ceiling insulation over-zealously installed to the eaves, so that it restricted roof-space ventilation. It can be seen why the prevalence of 'problem condensation' is greatest in 'improved dwellings' – especially those built or refurbished between the 1940s and the 1980s, when the twin risks of stiller air and cold surfaces multiplied.

In the 1950s, a typically improved house might have tighter-fitting windows and its loft insulated with 25mm (1in) of insulation quilt laid between the joists. With ceiling temperatures slightly raised by the insulation, and ventilation reduced by restriction of draughts, walls and single-glazed windows become the condensation targets, and an industry developed supplying devices to soak up or collect condensate from dripping windows.

In the 1960s, an equivalent refurbishment might include metal-framed double-glazed windows, transferring condensation from glass to frames and giving rise to pattern staining on upstairs ceilings, where the joists projecting above the 50mm (2in) insulation act as 'cold bridges' and attract condensation in stripes on the ceiling.

In the 1970s and 80s, refurbishments and new houses increasingly included cavity wall insulation, as well as PVC or timber-framed windows and double-glazing, as well as gradually increasing thicknesses of loft insulation. Once all these surfaces are insulated, condensation finds out the weak points, particularly at openings where window reveals and lintels still include no insulation.

A potentially troublesome fashion for recessed downlights – especially over bathrooms – started around this time and still continues. The downlight fitting usually has an open frame to avoid excess heat build-up, which encourages steam to rise rapidly into the loft-space above, where condensation can cause serious ceiling damage and electrical faults, as well as saturating insulation and potentially rotting timbers.

Good building practice, as researched and promoted by the BRE (Building Research Establishment), has included most of the current condensation-control measures since the 1980s; Part F2, which includes measures to reduce condensation, was introduced to the Building Regulations in 1985.

Diagnosis and Symptoms

The commonest visible symptom of interior condensation is mould, typically a grey or black speckle that is densest in the areas most affected. Although condensation does occur at low levels on walls, it is less common than at high levels. Low-level symptoms can be confused with those of rising damp, though close examination will usually show that rising-damp effects come from within the wall, so that decorative finishes are often distorted or disrupted from underneath rather than (initially at least) in themselves.

Surface Effects

In contrast, condensation symptoms occur on the surface and even serious cases of mould can often be cleaned off leaving the decorations still intact underneath. Provided that other measures to control the condensation are taken, this often means that the grim

appearance of interior surfaces, widely speckled with black mould, can be quickly restored to an acceptable state simply by cleaning with diluted bleach or similar mild fungicides. However, only in the mildest or intermittent cases will such cleaning alone be sufficient to ward off the return of the mould, if the condensation feeding it is not tackled.

Coldest Surfaces and Stillest Air

Compared to other forms of dampness, the visible symptoms of interior condensation tend to be associated with the coldest, most impervious surfaces and the stillest air. Sometimes, particularly around windows, these two factors counteract each other: while single-glazing is usually the coldest surface in a room in winter, single-glazed windows are often poorly fitting and draughty, which can reduce the amount of condensation or help its later evaporation. Once such windows are sealed up or simply draft-stripped, condensation may well increase and the still air within the window alcove, particularly if isolated from the room by curtains or blinds, will exacerbate this.

Another small but particularly cold surface that can lead to surprising amounts of concentrated condensation is a cold-water pipe passing through a steamy room, such as a bathroom or kitchen. Since such pipework is often concealed in boxings or cupboards,

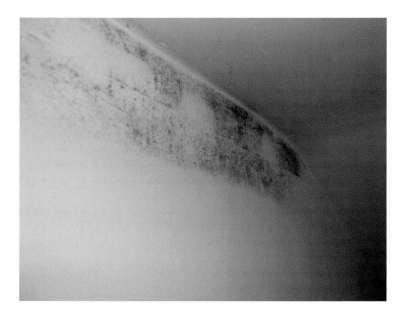

Fig 116 The speckled mould symptoms of interior condensation.

Fig 117   Areas most prone to condensation after double-glazing installed are parts of walls closest to the exterior or where air movement is least.

condensation may occur unnoticed for years – perhaps until damp patches appear on the ceiling below or the smell of mould in a cupboard leads to discovery. The symptoms of condensation on pipework can easily be mistaken for a plumbing leak, but close examination will show up the widespread surface dew rather than a single leak point.

Once double-glazing is installed, the next coldest surfaces will probably be the wall, ceiling and even floor surfaces closest to the exterior, typically the interior faces of window lintels, window reveals and floor thresholds at doorways.

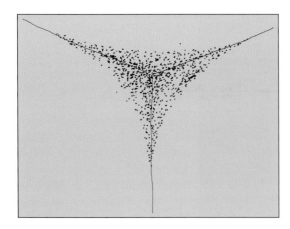

Fig 118   Classic 'three crescents' pattern of condensation mould growth in ceiling corners.

Fig 119   Sharply defined areas of condensation mould can show up construction faults, as here where the builder has left out the cavity insulation when he fitted a new cavity tray for the conservatory roof.

For houses without wall insulation, meaning most of those with solid walls built before 1900, the entire interior surface of external walls may be at risk, but the areas most liable to condensation will be the corners, alcoves, voids, cupboards and spaces between furniture and external walls, where air moves least and both ventilation and convection currents from radiators do not reach. There is a classic three-crescent pattern of condensation-derived mould that is often seen in corners at ceiling level, which directly reflects the limits of air movement.

Fault Finding

For houses with cavity walls, and even insulated cavity walls, condensation can often be a 'fault finder' indicating where there is 'cold bridging' or cavity insulation has been missed. The photograph (*see* Fig 119) shows a bathroom wall, where the installation of a cavity tray above a new conservatory roof led to the builders failing to replace the insulation in the cavity, leading to the conspicuous mould at high level. Similar tell-tale signs of localized condensa-

tion on ceilings could mean partially missing loft insulation.

Cold Bridges

Although building regulations have required 'cold-bridge insulation' around all openings in cavity walls – whether or not the cavity itself is insulated – since 1995 (Part L1), there are huge numbers of older cavity-walled houses that have had their inner-leaf walls returned tight to the outer leaf at every window and door: despite the DPC, which prevents penetrating damp reaching the interior at these points, the masonry and mortar readily conducts external cold to the interior and this frequently leads to condensation.

Less frequently, and more often in modern housing than in traditional dwellings, there can be 'structural cold bridges'; for example, where a concrete balcony is built into an external wall and the concrete may be cantilevered directly from the concrete floor slab, or where a steel beam is fixed through an external wall, perhaps to support an outside fire-escape staircase. The external side of these may be conspicuous

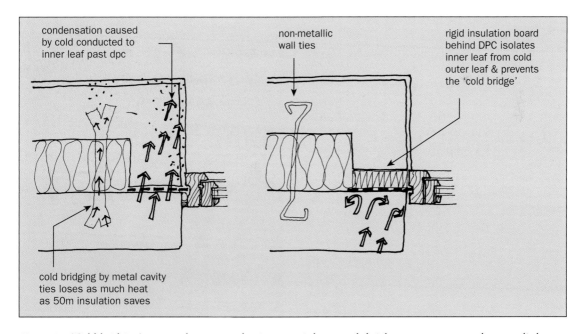

Fig 120   *'Cold bridging' occurs wherever conductive materials – metal, brick, stone, concrete and so on – link outside to inside: its symptoms are clearest for isolated occurrences in warm interiors.*

but they may be hidden internally until the condensation and mould shows them up.

Vapour Sources Past and Present
Another conspicuous characteristic of severe condensation and mould growth is its association with vapour sources, most typically in kitchens, utility rooms and bathrooms, and especially in shower rooms. Severe occurrence in these rooms may therefore be readily explained and expected, but there can be other unexpected and temporary vapour sources in other rooms, which can have a similar effect, such as flueless paraffin or bottled-gas heaters or even an habitually located kettle or the regular drying of clothes on racks or in tumble dryers. If the actual source of the vapour has been removed with a previous owner or tenant, it may be difficult to explain the symptoms of a condensation problem that has lost its cause.

Remedial Measures

Although individual cases should follow the diagnosis, the general sequence of remedial measures should be:

1. Reduce the amount of moisture vapour.
2. Extract or vent residual vapour near to its source.
3. Improve insulation of surfaces affected.
4. Improve surface absorption.
5. Improve level and distribution of heating.
6. Improve level and distribution of ventilation.

1.   Reducing Generation and Spread of Water Vapour
There are many basic practical measures, including cooking with lids on pans, using mixer taps to reduce steam, keeping water-storage tanks covered and closing doors while showering, cooking or drying clothes, so that moisture can be extracted or at least contained where it is generated rather than spread through potentially more vulnerable parts of the house.

2.   Venting or Extracting Vapour Near Its Source
Mechanical or passive extract vents in kitchens and bathrooms, even with windows, have been part of Building Regulations since 1985 (Part F1). Cooker hoods and bathroom extract fans have become common currency. Re-circulating cooker hoods that filter fumes but do not extract to the outside will not reduce water vapour and, accordingly, these do not meet building regulations for new or altered housing.

Extract fans can be controlled by adjustable timers to 'run on' after a room is used, or by passive infra-red people-detectors, though this is less common in houses than in commercial or public buildings; or most efficiently by humidistats, which switch on the fans only when there is excess humidity. Several manufacturers have improved the energy efficiency of their fans in recent years.

Passive stack ventilation will be less familiar to many people in its modern guise, though it is a permitted alternative to mechanical extract fans under Building Regulations (Part F2). As its name implies, a passive stack system uses no power to extract. Passive stacks are really small chimneys that use the natural 'stack effect' of warm air's tendency to rise to promote ventilation through vertical or near vertical pipe ducts from ceiling level to high-level external vents, usually at or near the ridge of a pitched roof.

Several manufacturers offer a kit of parts, including the external terminals, ductwork and internal vents, which can be sensitive to humidity, such that they open fully as water vapour is generated and close, usually to a 'trickle vent' status, once it is dispersed. It is important that ductwork passing through unheated areas, such as roof-spaces, is insulated, otherwise vapour will condense in the duct before it is vented.

Fig 121   Humidity-sensitive passive-stack ventilation extract grille. (Passivent Ltd)

3. *Improving Surface Insulation*

Insulating cold internal surfaces is effective in preventing condensation on that surface but, unless other measures are taken, or the insulation process is extensive and complete, condensation may simply be diverted to other surfaces that are still cold. Although the most effective measures involve a substantial thickness of insulation applied outside the internal surface, such as in loft or cavity wall insulation, these improvements may not be available, in solid stone-walled houses, for example, and internal lining may be needed.

Internal linings range from expanded polystyrene 'wallpaper' on a roll, only 3mm ($\frac{1}{8}$in) thick, applied with adhesive as an insulating underlayer to wallpaper or paint, through various grades and thicknesses of laminated insulation (12–55mm/$\frac{1}{2}$– $2\frac{1}{5}$in) and plasterboard (usually 9mm/$\frac{3}{8}$in) to semi-structural linings of timber battens or studs with insulation quilt between them and a plasterboard lining to the inside face. These linings can be applied to ceilings as well as walls.

The 3mm ($\frac{1}{8}$in) insulating wallpaper makes a slight, but potentially sufficient, difference to wall temperatures to be effective in mild cases. The more substantial linings can raise solid-wall insulation standards to match current building regulations and completely cure even severe interior condensation but they can create the risk of interstitial condensation instead, unless they incorporate an effective vapour check on the warm inner side of the insulation. Some, but not all, commercially available laminates of plasterboard and insulation do include such a vapour check at the interface between plasterboard and insulation. In more severe situations, it may be appropriate to mastic point the board joints before plastering or decorating. It is important to be aware that some insulating foam boards are twice as effective as others. So for example, a laminate that includes a 50mm (2in) layer of phenolic foam will provide as much insulation as 100mm (4in) of expanded polystyrene: although the more effective foam boards will be more expensive, the space saving can be particularly important on a domestic scale.

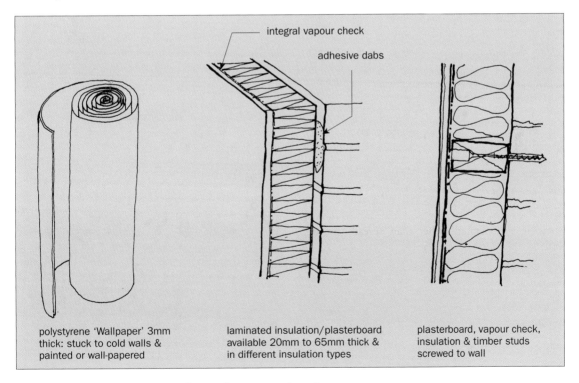

integral vapour check

adhesive dabs

polystyrene 'Wallpaper' 3mm thick: stuck to cold walls & painted or wall-papered

laminated insulation/plasterboard available 20mm to 65mm thick & in different insulation types

plasterboard, vapour check, insulation & timber studs screwed to wall

Fig 122   Internal insulation to reduce or eliminate condensation.

For houses whose exteriors are already painted or rendered, or can be clad without spoiling their appearance, external wall insulation, though generally more expensive, may be preferred as less disruptive internally and more effective in retaining the thermal mass of the walls as available to stabilize internal temperatures. Types of external insulation include various grades of foam boards and mineral fibre batts, usually clad in a fabric or metal mesh, and rendered with either a traditional two-coat render or, more often with proprietary systems, a thin, pre-mixed acrylic coating over a fabric reinforcement that may be less than 5mm ($\frac{1}{5}$ in) thick. It has to be remembered that the complexities of external insulation may include extending window sills, relocating rainwater pipes, extending the eaves and verges of roofs, and perhaps even replacing window and door frames: these add to the substantial cost of scaffold access to make this usually the most expensive solution. Since many of these costs apply whatever thickness of insulation is applied, it is usually best value to include as much insulation as can be afforded.

The insulation of cold-water pipes in heated areas using pipe lagging is an effective means of preventing condensation. In severe cases, impervious lagging is used with all joints carefully taped, which can be an exacting task. Where access to some complex pipework may be difficult, it may be simpler and as effective to provide a vapour check around the duct or void containing the pipes, so as to isolate them from a bathroom, for example; though if maintenance or access to valves is needed, the vapour check may get disturbed.

4.   *Improving Surface Absorption*
One of the simplest measures, likely to be effective only in mild cases, is to apply an anti-condensation paint whose finished texture allows the surface to trap condensation droplets for long enough on the surface to allow humidity to fall and the moisture to evaporate. More thorough measures of this kind would include replacing hard and relatively impermeable finishes, such as dense plaster or ceramic tiling, with more absorptive *in situ* materials like clay or lime plasters, or panels of cork or low-density fibre boards, which would also have an insulating effect but might not be so easy to clean and maintain in humid situations.

Some walling materials themselves, such as rammed earth or cob, and the less dense bricks and stones, can be left exposed, or re-exposed, rather than plastered or painted, to provide a naturally decorative and porous surface; though again, cleaning may be more difficult.

5.   *Improving Level and Distribution of Heating*
Partially or intermittently heated houses are more vulnerable to condensation because some surfaces will either be permanently cold or intermittently cold between heating periods. The level of heating required to prevent condensation is simply enough to keep internal surface temperatures above the dewpoint temperature of the air. As would be expected, the risk of condensation in a well-insulated house is very low, and the air temperatures can be allowed to fall outside periods of use; whereas a poorly insulated house built in thermally massive masonry has to be maintained at a higher temperature, more steadily, to avoid condensation from similar occupancy and activities. The effective distribution of heating depends partly on the heating system used and partly on the sub-division, shape and details of the interior.

The most distributive heating systems use large, low-temperature radiant panels, usually in floors but also possible in ceilings and walls. Since heat is radiated outwards from the heating surface, and then reflected back from opposite and adjacent surfaces, very effective coverage is achieved. Because the surfaces themselves are warmed, the chances of condensation are drastically reduced.

Warm-air heating systems, if well designed in an appropriate house, can also achieve good distribution, though there is more risk of voids, corners and storage areas remaining outside the flow of warm air. Traditional metal 'radiators', despite their name, work more effectively as convectors than radiators. By their nature, they are intermittently placed and there is often some risk of 'cold spots' outside the radiators' range. The longer the radiator, the wider will be its heat distribution, with 'skirting radiators' – again working very largely by convection – being the best example.

It should be remembered that the biggest 'radiator' for any house is the sun, and that improving a house's potential for receiving winter solar heat gain, and in turn using that heat gain to generate stack ventilation,

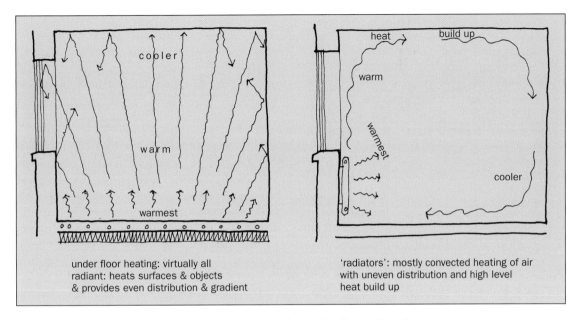

under floor heating: virtually all
radiant: heats surfaces & objects
& provides even distribution & gradient

'radiators': mostly convected heating of air
with uneven distribution and high level
heat build up

Fig 123   Heating methods: the wider the distribution, the less the chance of condensation.

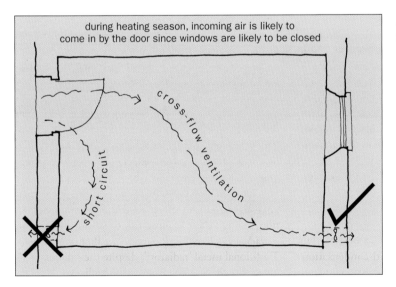

during heating season, incoming air is likely to
come in by the door since windows are likely to be closed

cross-flow ventilation

short circuit

Fig 124   Effective ventilation to minimize condensation.

can contribute significantly to a comfortable interior and to freedom from condensation.

6.   Improving Level and Distribution of Ventilation
Deliberately mentioned last, this measure carries with it other risks, particularly increased heat loss and, potentially, in some weather conditions, additional moisture and therefore potentially *increased* condensation.

Provided that moisture sources, such as kitchens, shower rooms and so on, have their local vapour extracted at source, only a modest air-change rate, typically between half and one air change per hour, is needed to avoid condensation in most conditions. Most existing houses are so poorly sealed that they have unintended ventilation rates of five to ten times this rate or more.

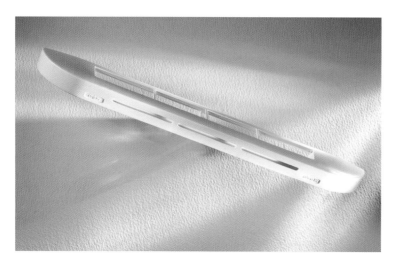

Fig 125   Trickle-vent fittings for window frames can be humidity-sensitive so that they open as humidity rises, allowing ventilation to increase. (Passivent Ltd)

Unfortunately, there is no well-distributed equivalent to under-floor heating in the world of domestic ventilation. Perhaps the closest parallel is a 'whole-house ventilation system': these sound more complicated than they are. The basic arrangement is one fan unit that extracts air via small ducts from kitchen, utility and bathroom(s), passes the air through a heat exchanger, so pre-warming the incoming fresh air, which it then discharges to living or circulation areas. The fan and heat-exchanger unit for a small house or flat will fit comfortably in a kitchen wall cupboard and the ducts can usually be accommodated within floor or wall structures. For the well-built or well-sealed house, these systems provide controllable levels of ventilation with very little heat loss and effective avoidance of condensation.

Where such an installation is not practical, there are simple rules to improving ventilation, such as allowing for 'through flow' so that there is both a way in for the air as well as a way out, and arranging the vent positions so that they clear the spaces rather than short-circuiting. If an extract fan is required in a room, it should be located opposite, rather than adjacent, to the source of incoming air, which in most cases during the heating season is the door into the room. To be most effective at removing vapour, ventilation needs to be provided close to the vapour source or at high level, since that is where the vapour will accumulate and is most likely to cause condensation.

The same suppliers that provide passive stack-ventilation systems offer vents for fitting through walls and roofs, and slot ventilators for incorporating in window frames or panes. These vents can be humidity sensitive so that they open as the humidity increases and close again as the humidity falls, helping to overcome the human factor that means windows get left open or closed too long, as well as allowing ventilation without loss of security.

INTERSTITIAL CONDENSATION

This hidden form of condensation can be innocuous – for example, in the case of the cavity wall described above, where it may occur harmlessly on the inner face of the outer leaf; or it may be disastrous – for example, where it occurs inside an unventilated timber-structured flat roof, leading to timber decay and structural collapse.

By their very nature, many of the 'in-between spaces' in the structures of our houses are both inaccessible to us and unseen by us but this does not mean they are inaccessible to water vapour, and as that water vapour permeates the layers of external structures, the temperature will drop until it reaches outside temperatures at or near the external surface of the house. During this drop in temperature, the water vapour will reach the dewpoint and condense. If this happens at or in a moisture-tolerant material, such as brickwork or stone, there may be no ill effects, but if

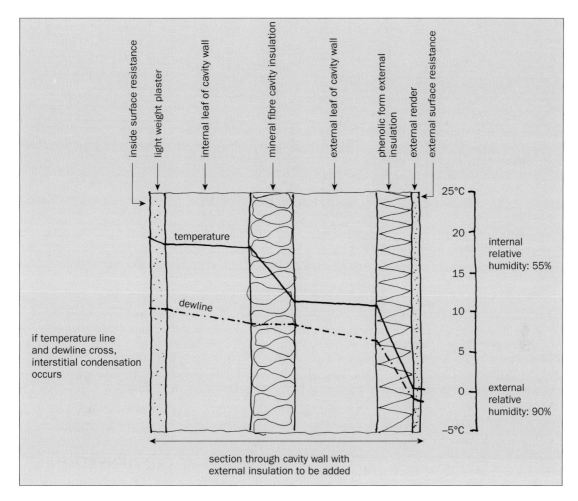

Labels on diagram (top):
inside surface resistance
light weight plaster
internal leaf of cavity wall
mineral fibre cavity insulation
external leaf of cavity wall
phenolic form external insulation
external render
external surface resistance

temperature

dewline

if temperature line and dewline cross, interstitial condensation occurs

25°C
20
15
10
5
0
–5°C

internal relative humidity: 55%

external relative humidity: 90%

section through cavity wall with external insulation to be added

Fig 126   Dewpoint diagram used to predict interstitial condensation.

it happens at or in timber or plaster or insulation, and if the dampness persists, these materials will deteriorate.

Dewpoint Diagram

The process is well illustrated in the dewpoint diagram, where temperature is plotted through a drawing of the external structure to check where the dewpoint occurs. If this happens (as would be indicated by the lines crossing) within the vulnerable parts of the structure, there is likely to be a condensation problem; whereas a dewpoint beyond these parts means condensation should give no trouble. Many insulation manufacturers will check a particular construction that is to incorporate their products,

producing a dewpoint calculation to advise purchasers of any condensation risk.

Tolerance and Permeability

Traditionally, as we have seen, there was less likelihood of condensation, and house structures tended to be both damp-tolerant and air-permeable. Traditional masonry walls 'breathe': they absorb internal moisture, which then evaporates from their surfaces, so that condensation occurring within the masonry will gradually evaporate from its surface. Similarly, traditional timber-clad and timber-framed houses are both permeable in the timber itself and usually still permeable in the assembly of other materials.

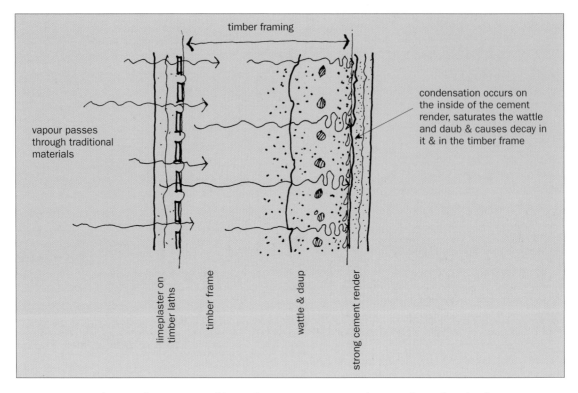

Fig 127   Decay from condensation caused by applying strong cement render to traditional timber frame construction.

A classic example of an interstitial condensation problem in a timber-framed house would be where an external wall has been rendered (probably in a misguided attempt to reduce penetrating damp) in a strong cement render, which is relatively impermeable to water vapour. Since the render is on the cold face of the wall, it forms a cold barrier to migrating moisture vapour, which condenses and then cannot evaporate. Consequently, moisture builds up to saturate the timber frame and promote decay.

Condensation in Pitched Roofing

A more widespread example occurs in early loft conversions to houses that have had their roofs protected by bituminous sarking felt below the tiles or slates. In order to make the most of the loft space, the loft room plasterboard was fixed to the underside of the rafters and, to reduce heat loss, the spaces between the rafters were filled with insulation, usually glass or mineral fibre quilt. All three measures – the sarking felt, the insulation and the sloping ceilings to maximize loft space – make good sense in themselves but applied together they will almost certainly lead to interstitial condensation. Just as it has always done, water vapour from the house will permeate through the ceilings and, just as it has done since the sarking felt was applied, some of it will condense on the underside of the felt, but now, instead of evaporating into the draughty openness of the roof-space, it drips into the insulation, which it saturates; in turn dampening the joists, staining ceilings and eventually leading to timber decay.

There are three measures to overcome this problem whether in new or refurbished houses: sarking, vapour check and ventilation.

Sarking
The first is in the sarking material under the tiles: instead of an impervious bitumen felt, a vapour-permeable sarking is used, which sheds any rainwater

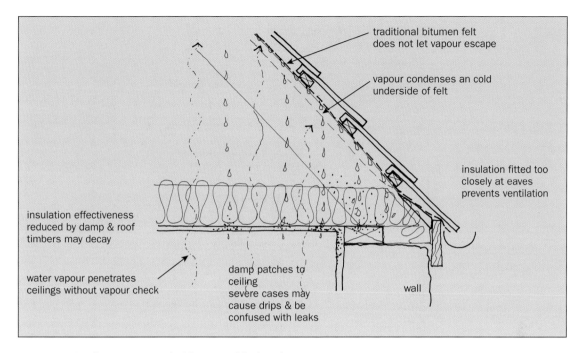

traditional bitumen felt
does not let vapour escape

vapour condenses an cold
underside of felt

insulation fitted too
closely at eaves
prevents ventilation

insulation effectiveness
reduced by damp & roof
timbers may decay

water vapour penetrates
ceilings without vapour check

damp patches to
ceiling
severe cases may
cause drips & be
confused with leaks

wall

Fig 128   Condensation in pitched bitumen-felted roofs.

that penetrates the tiles in the same way as the bitumen felt but still allows water vapour to evaporate through it. These sarking materials are now widely available at builders' merchants and generally accepted by building inspectors.

Vapour Check

The second is in the discouragement of vapour from passing through the ceiling by the use of a vapour check, usually a clear polythene sheeting, fixed to the underside of the rafters (after the insulation is fitted between them) before the plasterboard is fixed. I say 'discouragement', rather than prevention, and vapour 'check', rather than barrier because its very important that we are realistic about vapour control. The very process of fixing the vapour-check sheeting itself, and then the plasterboard over it, penetrates the polythene with hundreds of small holes occupied by the staples and nails; wherever light-fittings are fixed and cables brought through the ceiling, there is another path for vapour.

It is sometimes suggested that foil-backed plasterboard is an acceptable substitute for a polythene vapour check. Although aluminium foil does have

excellent vapour resistance, the foil backing to plasterboard is seldom an equivalent measure and should not be relied upon unless all board joints are foil-taped on the rear face – a difficult operation to do well – and the boards' foil faces are installed in perfect condition, rather than frequently scratched and pierced, as so easily happens on site. Even where workmanship is good, the vapour control will not be complete.

In cases where the ceiling is already in place and not due to be renewed, vapour resistance can be improved by decorating with oil-based paints, such as eggshell – although even three coats will not provide the vapour resistance of polythene sheeting.

Ventilation

The third measure is in ensuring good ventilation of the cold side of the insulation. This is treated differently where bituminous sarking is retained in place, in which case a minimum air gap of 50mm (2in), vented top and bottom, has to be retained between the upper surface of the insulation and the underside of the sarking. This provides sufficient airflow to clear

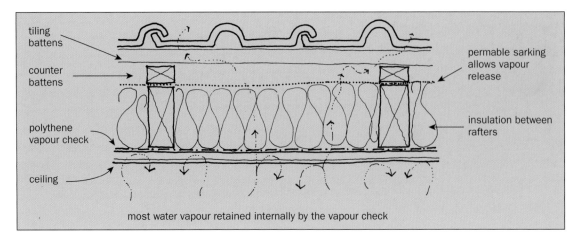

Fig 129   Vapour control and dispersal in pitched roof and ceiling spaces.

the condensation from the sarking and allow the insulation and the rafters to remain dry, or at least to dry out in between condensation occurrences. In new construction or where the roof covering is refurbished or renewed, the sarking will be the vapour-permeable kind laid directly over the insulation, without sagging between the rafters. To allow any water penetrating the tiles to drain away freely and to ensure good ventilation under the tiles, the tiling battens are raised by 'counter-battens' – usually 25mm (1in) thick – fixed above the rafters.

Condensation in Flat Roofs

A more severe and less easily resolved version of this problem occurs in flat roofs. By their nature, flat-roofing materials are both waterproof and continuous: being flat, they cannot rely on the shedding principle of loosely overlapping scales, as do most domestic pitched-roofing materials. So, whether the flat roof is covered in lead, bitumen felt, asphalt or a single-ply membrane, it is generally impervious to both rain from the outside and virtually impervious to vapour from within.

Cold Roofs

To make matters worse, flat roof structures – especially on small house roofs or extensions – are often of minimal depth, perhaps using joists only 100 or 150mm deep (4 or 6in), and because they are flat, there is no natural air current promoted in the void

between the joists. Finally, the typical edge details of flat roofing are generally sealed with no natural ventilation paths for air to flow in and out of the joist voids.

Current good practice – and building regulations – for flat roofing dictates that at least two opposite sides of the roof have fly-screened ventilation openings equivalent to a continuous gap of 25mm (1in); a minimum 50mm (2in) gap above the insulation below the roof deck allows air to circulate.

With small joists and this 50mm air gap, insulation often has to be fitted at least partly under the joists, and if this is done with a laminated insulation/plasterboard, the material should incorporate a vapour check between the plasterboard and the insulation. Otherwise, and in the case of deeper joists that can accommodate both the air gap and an adequate insulation depth, a vapour check should be fixed to the underside of the joists before the ceiling is fixed. This arrangement of insulation at the inside is referred to as a 'cold roof' since the roof-deck and part of the structure is outside the insulation and therefore cold.

Warm Roofs

Another approach to flat roofing is to fit the insulation and the vapour check above the structure, which avoids the condensation problem and is referred to as a 'warm roof' detail, since the structure and roof-deck are all kept warm by the insulation. Since traditional felt flat roofs are short-lived, this can be a practical

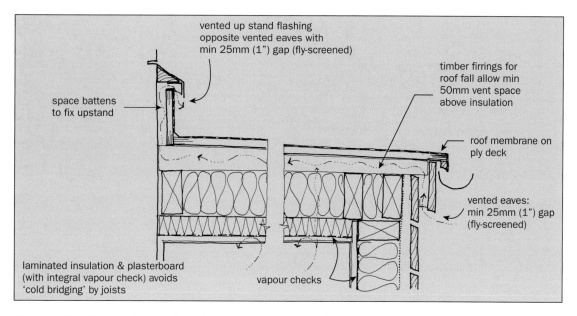

Fig 130   'Cold' flat roofing: condensation control by vapour check and cross-ventilation.

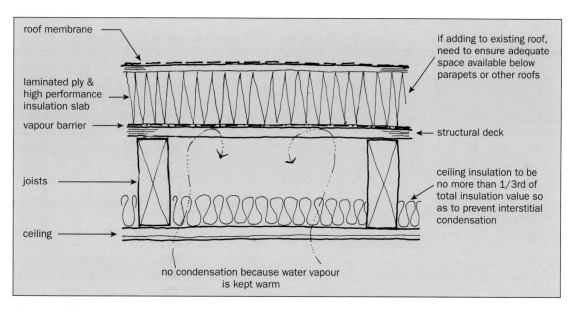

Fig 131   'Warm' flat roof: insulation outside the structure avoids condensation without ventilation.

measure to combine with replacement of the roof covering, as long as there is sufficient height available above the roof to accommodate the insulation thickness. If the highest grade foam insulants, such as phenolic foam, are used laminated to plywood, the overall height of the flat roof would be increased by approximately 90mm ($3\frac{1}{2}$ in) to meet building regulations. Although in this situation up to a third of the insulation value in the roof could still be provided between the joists, the temptation to add more

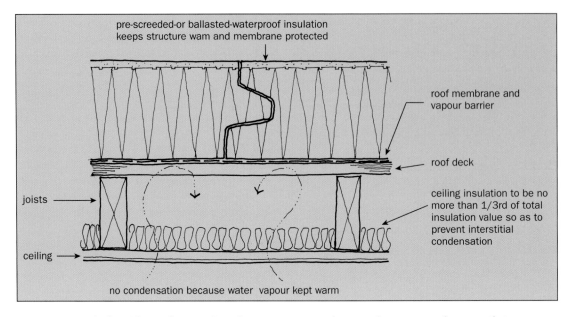

pre-screeded-or ballasted-waterproof insulation
keeps structure wam and membrane protected

roof membrane and
vapour barrier

roof deck

ceiling insulation to be no
more than 1/3rd of total
insulation value so as to
prevent interstitial
condensation

joists

ceiling

no condensation because water vapour kept warm

Fig 132 'Upside-down' flat roof: external insulation protects membrane and structure without ventilation.

insulation below must be avoided, otherwise the dew-point will be brought within the roof structure again. It is important that the over-deck insulation is either vapour proof in itself or is laid over a vapour check.

Upside-Down Roofs
Finally, the Rolls Royce of flat-roofing details is to insulate outside the membrane in what is known as an 'upside-down roof'; this not only maintains the complete roof structure within the insulated envelope but also protects the roof membrane itself against both temperature changes and physical damage. Such details are often used under roof gardens, where the physical protection is especially valuable and where the increase in height can be absorbed within the garden build-up. Insulation materials suitable for this detail have to be impermeable, closed-cell foam boards and since they are normally loose-laid, they need to be restrained against wind uplift by a heavy layer of gravel or pavings, usually about 50mm (2in) thick. Dow Building Products' Styrofoam Roofmate range includes an interlocking and screed-surfaced insulation slab that avoids the need for heavy ballast, except to exposed perimeters, and is therefore especially useful for lightly structured domestic roofs.

Condensation in Wall Claddings

A similar problem to the flat-roof condensation risk can arise in walls externally clad with impervious materials: the cement-rendered timber-frame building referred to above is an example, but more severe problems can occur with metal or plastic claddings.

Metal claddings have not been used much on UK houses, although small numbers of metal-clad prefabricated houses remain from the 1940s and 1950s and there have been a few instances of the 'industrial aesthetic' of profiled metal creeping into housing design in the last few decades.

Plastic (usually uPVC) cladding has been marketed as a replacement for timber boarding, which it is usually designed to resemble. If these claddings are detailed and installed to allow good ventilation behind the plastic at top and bottom edges, there may be no problem; but if such claddings are installed to protect against driving rain in severely exposed locations, they may have been largely sealed at their edges and may cause condensation as a result.

Even the double skin or foamed cellular plastic claddings, which are advertised as improving insulation levels, may be subject to condensation; even more so if the wall they clad has been insulated internally or in its cavity.

Other cladding materials occasionally used in houses would include plywood and dense mineral fibre or calcium silicate pre-finished claddings, all of which would have high vapour-resistance and therefore be likely to cause condensation unless they had been installed to a freely ventilated rain screen detail.

Condensation in Floors

Although floors are a less obvious zone for condensation, the interstitial kind can cause serious problems here too, especially in floors that are suspended above ground level, perhaps over a ground-level ventilated void or above a passage or carport, which brings external air temperatures to the underside of the floor.

Timber Suspended Floors

If such suspended floors are timber, their original state will probably have been timber boards above the joists with no insulation or further protection. Although there may have been some condensation, it is very likely to have been ventilated away by the airflow beneath and through the floor. Once 'improvements' are made, the condensation situation may have been made worse; for example, if sheet floorings are laid over the boards to reduce the draughts, surface condensation may occur on the inside of this. If insulation is fitted between the joists to reduce heat loss, this is usually best as a fibrous material that can form a snug fit and reduce draughts as well, rather than rigid board material that may need very precise cutting to achieve a good fit. If insulation is not closely fitted, vapour flow and condensation may be concentrated in small areas to a worse degree. It is therefore best to combine floor insulation with a vapour-check polythene sheet laid above the joists and below the floor boards.

In supporting insulation between joists it is very important that any material used is thoroughly permeable. In laying insulation from above, a good method is to use a polypropylene netting (such as is used for protection of fruit bushes against birds), which is draped over the joists and stapled in place near the bottom of the joists.

If access is available from below, as in a cellar or undercroft, for example, plasterboard can be used if a

ceiling is required, though in a really cold cellar this would be advisable only if a vapour check were fitted above the insulation as well. Alternatively, one of the vapour-permeable reinforced roof sarkings may be simply stapled to the underside of the joists.

Care needs to be taken to ensure that the void below the floor is effectively cross-ventilated. If the suspended floor has been 'cut off' from ventilation on one side (for example, by a later concrete-floored extension), it may be necessary to provide ventilation ducts around or below the obstruction, or to install a vertical vent pipe or even an extract fan.

Concrete Suspended Floors

The same problems can occur with concrete suspended floors, whether these are solid concrete or 'beam and block' or 'beam and pot'. These latter types of suspended floor were increasingly used as ground floors in houses built in the second-half of the twentieth century, especially on sloping sites or over poor ground conditions. Upgrading of these floors tends to be more difficult because there is no void to insulate, though they are seldom as draughty as the basic timber joisted and boarded floor.

If access is available to the underside, it may be possible to fix insulation there, which avoids disturbing internal floor finishes, but it is important that support for the insulation is vapour permeable. Alternatively, it may be necessary to install insulation above the concrete floor, usually as a floating floor of a boarded deck over insulation boards. Despite the disruption this will cause internally, it is essential in this case to install a polythene vapour-check over the insulation and under the new boarding. If a floating floor has already been installed and condensation is suspected, it may be due to the omission of this essential vapour check.

Solid Ground Floors

Although solid concrete or stone floors are less liable to condensation than suspended versions, there is still this possibility, especially at the floor's external perimeter and particularly when internal floor level is above external ground levels, allowing heat to transfer through floor and wall directly to the outside.

Only since 1990 has it been required under Building Regulations(Part L1) to incorporate insulation

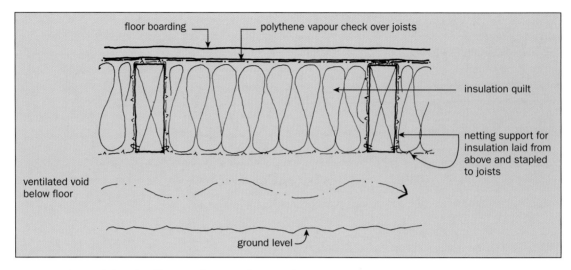

Fig 133 *Suspended timber floor: insulation without condensation.*

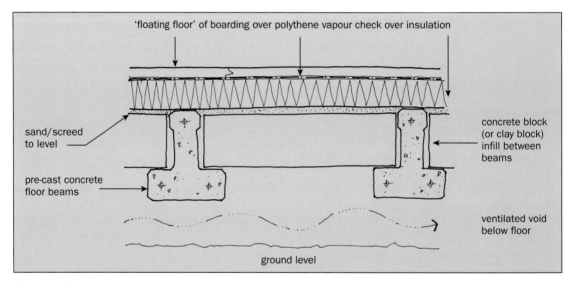

Fig 134 *Suspended concrete floor: insulation without condensation.*

in ground floors. Where ground floors are replaced, a common part of refurbishment in derelict houses, there is a choice in placing the insulation either below a new concrete slab or above a slab and below a screed or timber deck, as in the floating floor example described above.

It is seldom advantageous for the householder to have insulation above the slab, whether this is below a screed or a floating floor, and it is usually more expensive both financially and environmentally. Although many builders prefer to lay a rough slab at an earlier stage as a working platform, they are unlikely to offer this version at less cost since it involves more material and more labour. Our preferred specification is to lay the insulation directly over the DPM and then to lay the floor slab above a polythene vapour-check, which also serves to keep the wet concrete out of the insulation boards. To allow for the laying of

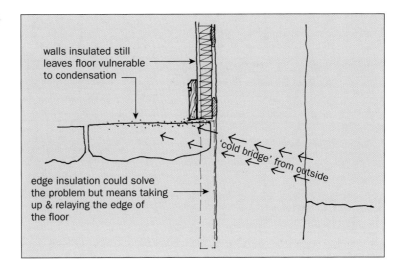

Fig 135   Floor condensation with low ground levels: can be confused with rising or penetrating damp.

walls insulated still leaves floor vulnerable to condensation

'cold bridge' from outside

edge insulation could solve the problem but means taking up & relaying the edge of the floor

concrete, this vapour check is laid in the same 250 or 300micron polythene as the DPM, as opposed to the 125micron polythene vapour-checks used at less vulnerable ceiling levels.

If floors are not being replaced, it is possible to insulate the perimeter by excavating a narrow trench and inserting closed-cell insulation boards vertically;

in conjunction with wall insulation, this should prevent condensation at this level.

Chimney Condensation

This could rank as a hybrid form – within the structure, yet on the inside surface of the flue. Burning fossil fuels releases large quantities of water vapour: every

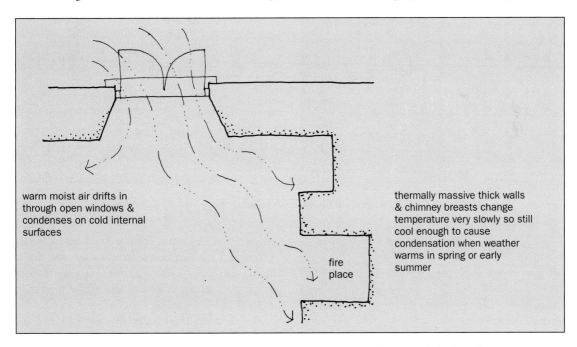

warm moist air drifts in through open windows & condenses on cold internal surfaces

fire place

thermally massive thick walls & chimney breasts change temperature very slowly so still cool enough to cause condensation when weather warms in spring or early summer

Fig 136   Internal 'summer condensation': common in traditional masonry houses with thick walls – especially in less heated rooms.

kilogram of hydrogen in the fuel combines with oxygen from air to produce 9kg (9ltr) of water vapour. Apart from the direct problem of damp and staining from flue condensate, there is the additional problem of acidic corrosion from the flue gas (carbon dioxide and sulphur dioxide) dissolved in the condensate, that then eats into mortar in masonry flues and damages brick or stonework. Prevention can be achieved by lining flues in rebated clay or stainless steel, though once this sort of corrosion is advanced, chimneys may need to be rebuilt.

Summer Condensation

Finally, a word about 'summer condensation': both interior and interstitial condensation can occur 'in reverse' during warm weather and this can lead to confusing symptoms that may be mistaken for other forms of damp, simply because of the weather conditions or time of year. The most obvious form is interior condensation on thermally massive surfaces, typically chimney

Fig 137   Test for condensation – rather than rising or penetrating damp.

breasts and thick internal walls in traditional buildings, that often retain their low temperatures well into the summer months. During warm humid weather, vapour in the external air drifting through open windows condenses on these cold internal surfaces producing the characteristic 'sweating' – fine droplets beading on the surface, which can easily be mistaken for rising damp, although it is seldom concentrated at low levels and will tend to show a dry surface beneath if it is wiped away. A sure test, if in doubt, is to wipe away the moisture from a patch of wall and tape a patch of polythene or aluminium foil tightly to the wall: after a few hours, if the patch is dry on its exposed face but wet on the face taped to the wall, the damp is coming from the wall. On the other hand, if the exposed face of the patch is wet, the damp is from condensation. It may also be damp on both faces of course, in which case both forms of dampness may be present.

Less obvious and less common is interstitial summer condensation. This is typical in a dry-lined south-facing masonry wall, where moisture in the wall is heated by the sun and driven inwards – as well as evaporating outwards – where it meets the cooler outer face of the drylining, which may have a vapour check, and condenses. Drylining is often relatively vulnerable to damp and symptoms may show in staining or in dampness at the base of the wall or decay in the skirting boards, which is again easily confused with other sources of dampness that are often much more difficult to diagnose. If the outer masonry includes a cavity, a severe problem may be eased by improving ventilation to it at high and low level, so as to clear the vapour before it reaches the cool interior. Unfortunately, in winter, that same ventilation of the cavity will increase heat loss and may increase winter condensation by cooling the outer face of the inner leaf, though this in itself is less likely to be a serious problem than the interior condensation to the drylining.

Remedial Measures Summary

So, to reiterate the measures available to cure or reduce interstitial condensation are:

- Reduce vapour at source, by avoidance or extraction.
- Reduce the vapour's passage through the construction by installing a vapour-check material or coating on the warm inside surface.

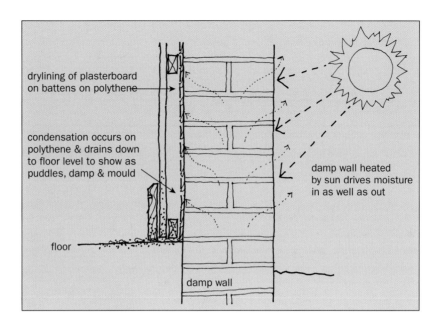

Fig 138   Interstitial summer condensation behind drylining: can be confused with rising or penetrating damp but should be short term.

drylining of plasterboard on battens on polythene

condensation occurs on polythene & drains down to floor level to show as puddles, damp & mould

floor

damp wall heated by sun drives moisture in as well as out

damp wall

• Avoid or remove impermeable materials in the cold outer parts of the construction, so that vapour has a chance to ventilate externally and any condensation that does occur has a chance to evaporate.

• Where permeable materials cant be used- such as in flat roofs, either allow air-space and edge details to ventilate between the insulation and the roof deck, or insulate above the roof deck in a fully bonded sandwich of insulation and membrane (a 'warm roof') or above the membrane itself in an 'upside-down roof'.

• For solid floors, where there is no ventilation available to the cold side of the insulation, the vapour check is essential, otherwise the insulation may become saturated and less effective, as well as becoming a source of damp with symptoms similar to rising damp.

CHAPTER 5

Leaking Services

Although the effects of long-term leaks from services can be as destructive as any other form of dampness, once diagnosed, the stopping of the leaks is usually straightforward. Technological progress has brought these problems with it: the primitive hut had no 'services', with no water pipes or drains indoors and no gutters or drains on the outside.

WASTE-PIPES AND RAINWATER GOODS

Externally, diagnosis is simplified because both soil and waste-pipes and 'rainwater goods' – the generic term applied to gutters and downpipes – are generally visible, though there are exceptions where rash or inexperienced designers or builders have concealed downpipes within walls, usually to avoid their visual disruption of a facade. I have worked on a church where the large entrance canopy roof is drained to a 25mm (1in) downpipe embedded in the front wall of the church. Naturally, such a small pipe had blocked, so that the canopy roof simply sheds its rain around its perimeter. Clearing a small, embedded pipe is difficult and a short-lived solution, so the congregation simply gets used to dodging the 'rain curtain' as they go in.

Provided there is good access to both ends of a concealed downpipe, and neither joints nor corrosion along its length, in theory there is no reason why it should not perform well in the long term; but mercifully their occurrence in houses is rare.

The other simplifying factor in diagnosing rainwater goods leakage is that any persistent leak almost invariably leaves obvious traces: the classic symptoms

Fig 139   Embedded and undersized rainwater pipe is permanently blocked.

of leaking downpipes are either scoured clean vertical streaks on masonry around the pipe, or local moss growth in much the same pattern. The two photographs on page 121 are from the same church: the scouring is on the south side, where sunlight is too much for the moss; whereas on the shady north side, the moss thrives.

Fig 140   Wall around a rainwater pipe scoured clean signifies a long-term blockage.

Fig 141   Moss growth around a pipe on a shaded wall is an equivalent sign of blockage.

Leaking gutters can produce similar local signs on a smaller scale from faulty joints, cracks or breaks. Soil and waste-pipes seldom produce such clear marks because flow, and therefore leakage, tends to be brief and intermittent.

There is a tendency to replace defective rainwater goods rather than repair them, usually based on the labour cost of repair and redecoration exceeding the purchase cost of replacements. Huge quantities of cast-iron rainwater goods have been scrapped and replaced with uPVC on this premise.

Cast Iron

Although the cast iron may have lasted more than a century with relatively little maintenance, and the performance of uPVC rainwater goods often begins to deteriorate after only thirty years, the strict financial equation may still be correct. One of the principal reasons why builders assume they will need to scrap the cast iron is that to remove it for full refurbishment

is difficult without breaking the joints. However, there are repair kits for sealing and patching guttering *in situ*, which comprise a liquid plastic repair compound combined with a flexible reinforcement mesh. Provided such repairs are carefully prepared and well done, they can extend the life of cast-iron guttering for a similar period to the life of a uPVC replacement, and quite possibly at much less cost, since there is no removal and replacement labour involved.

Downpipes, whether for rainwater or for soil and waste, are not so easy to repair, since the interior of the pipe is inaccessible. Failures in external cast-iron pipes often show in cracks, particularly around the joints; once such cracks show, usually through leak stains, paintwork cannot be well maintained. It is possible to make short-life cosmetic repairs, say in the course of repainting, by grinding out the surface of the crack and filling it with a plastic metal-repair compound, but replacement of the section of pipe containing the crack is recommended. Once a pipe

121

has cracked around its full circumference, it will be virtually impossible to repair on the wall side without removal. In some situations, this may involve dismantling of further sections of pipe and their wall brackets, with the attendant risk of further breakages. Builders genuinely cannot tell until the work is done how difficult dismantling like this is going to be, and how many sections of pipe or brackets may break in the process. Consequently it is hard for them to quote firm prices for such repairs – much harder than the relatively predictable alternative of removing and scrapping all the existing pipework and replacing in plastic. So, it is likely that such repairs will be limited to historic houses – where the only permitted renewal may be in new cast iron to match – and to houses whose owners are capable and ambitious enough to do some of the repairs, or at least dismantling, themselves; or confident enough to employ a builder on a time basis to do them.

Other materials than cast iron used for both soil and rainwater goods include asbestos cement, uPVC, aluminium, steel and, occasionally, pitch fibre, zinc, copper and lead.

Asbestos Cement

Asbestos cement was quite widely used for guttering, downpipes and flue pipes in the twentieth century. Although all asbestos materials need to be treated with care, asbestos cement is both the least dangerous and most common of those normally found in houses. Painted asbestos rainwater goods are not so obvious as the mottled matt grey of the raw material but in most cases, the thickness of the material – typically 6–10mm ($\frac{1}{4}$–$\frac{3}{8}$in) will show up at the joints and give it away. In most circumstances, there is little or no risk attached to its retention in pipes and guttering. However, care needs to be taken to avoid disturbing or damaging it in dry conditions; so, for example, clearing leaves out of asbestos cement guttering should be done in damp conditions, since it is in the abrasion, breakage or cutting of the material in dry conditions that asbestos dust and fibres may be released.

If, for whatever reason, it is decided to replace asbestos cement drainage or rainwater goods, the dismantling and removal should again be done in damp conditions, or, if dry, the work should be frequently sprayed with water to keep it damp.

Appropriate dust masks should be worn by those doing the work and the dismantled asbestos cement components need to be identified as such and wrapped up when they are transported for appropriate disposal.

The most likely situation where householders may find the more hazardous, fibrous types of asbestos is around an old boiler, either in the flue joints or in insulation of pipework or of the boiler itself, or occasionally in other forms of insulation: if there is any chance of these being present, it is advisable to obtain qualified advice before disturbing any of the material. Local authority environmental health officers may well be able to advise. If such material is present and is either in poor condition or needs to be disturbed to allow for replacement or alterations, then the work will need to be done by licensed contractors with fully protective precautions and disposal.

uPVC

Unplasticized polyvinyl chloride (uPVC) has come to dominate the UK rainwater goods, and soil and waste market, and has been widely marketed as both simple to install and maintenance-free. uPVC systems rely on the flexibility and spring of the material to allow snap-fit installation of gutters in brackets and joints. The joints are waterproofed by neoprene gaskets adhered or 'captive' in the recesses of the joint, which allow for the significant thermal movement of the plastic; soil and waste-pipes are also jointed via solvent adhesives, as well as with gaskets. White uPVC retains its appearance well, though it is the least resistant to ultraviolet degradation from sunlight. Grey, black and brown – and from some manufacturers a few other colours – have better ultraviolet resistance but are subject to gradual fading, which can lead to a patchy appearance after twenty years or so, especially for the darker colours on south facades. Ageing occurs in the plastic, making it less flexible, and there is some joint failure from perished gaskets; but generally the systems are relatively trouble-free.

Many houses may have a mixture of materials and in the course of repair, refurbishment or extension, it may be necessary to decide whether to replace like with like, or to renew all in one material. There are serious environmental drawbacks to the manufacture and disposal of PVC but these need to be set against

Fig 142   The faded appearance of the thirty-year-old black uPVC rainwater pipe contrasts with the shiny black of the new pipe below but it is still effective.

the environmental costs of alternatives, whether the repeated painting of cast iron or the manufacture and possible powder-coating of aluminium, for example. Each individual situation needs to be judged on its merits but, whenever usable materials are discarded, they should be re-used or recycled, if possible. Although formal recycling – particularly for plastics – can be difficult to arrange, the informal method of the 'freecycle' website or simply a sign reading 'help yourself' over a safely stacked pile of discarded materials can be surprisingly successful.

Aluminium

Aluminium can be used for rainwater goods either cast or roll-formed. Cast aluminium, powder-coated, can be an acceptable maintenance-free alternative to cast iron for historic buildings, since it is similar in appearance as well as being very robust; but in the case of a listed building, consent will be needed.

Drawn or roll-formed aluminium, usually also colour-coated, is much thinner – and therefore less robust – than cast and available in very long lengths, so is cheaper; though the manufacture limits the appearance to simpler shapes without the crisp detail of casting. Both types generally rely on gasketed joints, though cast systems can be mastic-jointed for a closer match to traditional cast iron. Uncoated aluminium, either plain 'mill-finished' or anodized, is simpler to recycle and, if not anodized, will gradually weather to a dull whitish grey.

Steel

Mild steel is galvanized and can be colour-coated as well. Although made in Scandinavia, and not as widely available as uPVC, it can be competitive in price, installation and life-span, as well as claiming better environmental credentials. Plain galvanized finishes are at risk from 'leaf tea corrosion', so alloyed or powder-coated finishes should always be applied to galvanized rainwater goods.'

Fig 143   Galvanized steel rainwater goods offer an environmental alternative to uPVC at similar cost.

123

Stainless steel, generally made from at least 70 per cent recycled material and with an extremely long life, is perhaps an ideal self-finished metal for rainwater goods but its high cost makes its use in most domestic situations unlikely, unless access difficulties make permanence more critical than materials cost, for high dormers perhaps.

Pitch Fibre

Pitch fibre is a bituminous material reinforced with cellulose fibres, which was widely used for cheap pipework and guttering, as well as corrugated roof sheeting. Due to its tendency to deform over time, it is no longer permitted for underground pipework.

For underground pipework, this can lead to serious deformation of the pipes and eventual collapse and blockage; but above ground, the same characteristics in guttering can lead to sagging – especially on south facades where the sun softens the bitumen – though downpipes tend to be less affected.

Where pitch-fibre pipes have deformed below ground – usually detected in a camera survey by a drainage specialist – there used to be no alternative to replacement, which should be in clay pipe with flexible joints for environmental reasons, as well as for maximum strength. Recently, however, drainage contractors have developed 'reforming' processes that reshape and then line the pipes with a resin liner, all without excavation.

For above-ground pitch-fibre pipework and guttering, total replacement may not be essential but there may be compatibility problems if guttering is replaced without downpipes.

Decoration

Decorative maintenance of traditionally painted drainage goods is straightforward – in theory – though often difficult in terms of access and preparation. Powder-coated metals should need no maintenance but if damaged, they can be touched up using compatible coatings from the manufacturer, if known, or from powder-coating specialists, if not. uPVC can be painted in order to mask fading but it may be difficult to achieve consistent adhesion, given the smooth surfaces and the degree of thermal movement in the plastic, and, once painted, the improved appearance lasts only as long as the paint.

Zinc

Zinc in rainwater goods and pipework is relatively rare in the UK, though common in mainland Europe. Although zinc for roofing and flashings is now made in relatively corrosion-resistant alloys, typically with titanium, isolated occurrences of older zinc in UK housing are likely to be in the basic metal, which is prone to corrosion, particularly in the more industrial areas with acidic air pollution. It is therefore likely that defective pipework or guttering in zinc will need complete replacement and, unless it is very recent and therefore alloyed, an early need for replacement should be assumed, even if it is not yet leaking.

Copper

Copper is marketed for rainwater goods but its use in housing is probably as rare as stainless steel, and at similar cost but shorter life, it would be selected for its appearance, if at all.

Lead

Lead in pipework is common in older housing, both in water-supply pipes and in smaller waste-pipes from sinks, baths and wash basins. It is much less common in rainwater goods to houses and is usually of eighteenth-century date or earlier, so tends to be associated with historic buildings. Since lead is such a stable material – especially where protected from temperature change – it tends to remain intact and operational for very long periods.

The most frequent problems with lead service pipework and rainwater goods are likely to be mechanical damage of external leadwork caused by vandalism or careless maintenance, shortage of lead-working skills needed to effect alterations without replacement, furring up of lead water-supply pipes in hard-water areas and concerns over lead contamination of water supplies in soft-water areas.

External leadwork services to historic buildings need to be treated with respect and proper craftsmanship. Although the cost of this may seem high, the very long life of these components, and their contribution to the character of the buildings they service, will easily repay the investment. The Lead Sheet Association provides both excellent detailed advice on correct craftsmanship and a nationwide list of competent lead specialists. For historic buildings, careful assessment of the existing situation is needed and advice from the local council's conservation officer should be sought.

Internal and below-ground lead pipework is being steadily replaced in the course of alterations and improvements and, although leadwork is seldom a cause of leakage and dampness in itself, its adaptation and combination with other materials has often led to unsatisfactory details, suggesting that replacement is often a better option than retention.

Internal Roof Gutters

One particular problem with internal leadwork, which proves the exception to this rule, is the internal gutter draining the valleys from 'M roofs'. This is common in larger Georgian and Regency terraced houses, where the roofs are constructed as two small pitched roofs whose ridges run parallel to front and back facades with an 'internal valley' between them. Where the front facade is parapetted, it was often considered aesthetically unacceptable to bring a rainwater pipe down the front facade, which meant that both the front parapet gutter and the central valley had to be drained internally or diverted to the rear facade. This diversion was achieved by forming a lead box gutter, often at a very shallow fall, across the ceilings to the rear gutter or downpipe. These open lead gutters were typically constructed from long lengths of lead simply folded into a trough and supported by timber boards below and to each side.

Unless the parapet and valley gutters are scrupulously maintained, there is a high risk of debris building up in the nearly flat internal gutters and rainwater overflowing onto the ceilings. Many repairs and 'improvements' after serious flooding incidents involved replacing the open lead gutters with plastic drainpipes, but this is an illusory substitute for good maintenance: any failure to keep the external gutters clear will again lead to build-up of debris in the internal pipes and, although they may not themselves flood, their blockage will simply lead to flooding of the parapet or valley gutters over the same ceilings. Because the replacement pipes are 'closed', they are not accessible for simple inspection, so maintenance is actually made more difficult.

PLUMBING AND HEATING LEAKS

Storage Tanks

Cold-water storage tanks, usually within roof-spaces of houses, were historically built *in situ* from timber, lined with lead sheet. Later, pre-fabricated tanks were assembled *in situ* from bolted or riveted cast iron or galvanized steel plates, both being subject to eventual corrosion. The difficulties of dismantling them has meant that many have been abandoned in attics long after their function has been superseded by replacement metal or later black polythene or fibreglass (GRP) tanks. Polythene and GRP are more or less permanent materials within a dark loft-space, safe from ultraviolet damage. The flexibility that allows new polythene tanks to be squeezed and distorted through surprisingly small access trapdoors, diminishes with

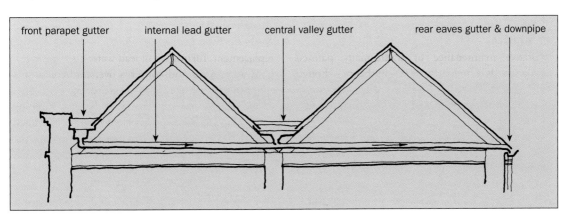

Fig 144 Internal loft gutters: open access allows for easy maintenance.

age and there can be a risk of damage and splitting in the course of handling stored goods through the loft. Similarly, supply and feed pipes, often poorly supported away from the tank wall, can cause distortion splits around flanges if the pipework is carelessly distorted or 'loaded'. Some polythene splits may be repairable with adhesive but replacement is more likely and reliable. GRP tanks are stiffer and more robust, less flexible and more costly.

Water Pipes: Furring Up and Corrosion

The build-up of mineral deposits on the inside of water-supply pipes, usually known as 'furring up', is common to any traditional pipework material that lasts a long time; most typically lead and cast or galvanized iron. Although mineral deposits occur in cold-water supply pipes, according to the mineral content of the local water supply, the most serious furring up occurs in hot-water systems supplying hard water from which the calcium salts are deposited as limescale – most obvious in our kettles but producing more serious problems in our pipework and hot-water tanks. There are electronic-, magnetic- and chemical-scale treatment units that can be fitted to mains supply pipes to reduce scale formation; these work by temporarily reducing the adhesive quality of the scale in the water, so that it tends to remain in suspension rather than build up on pipework and other surfaces. Water softeners change the chemical composition of the water by extracting scale-forming calcium and magnesium via a resin filter, which is then flushed with brine to reactivate it.

Once pipework is heavily furred up – from whatever cause – replacement is advisable. Water tanks and heat exchangers can be de-scaled but the process is laborious and there is a risk of damage. For domestic systems, therefore, replacement is likely to be more economic, alongside the installation of a scale-treatment device on the incoming main, so that the problem does not recur.

The converse of furring up in pipework – and more relevant to leaks and damp – is corrosion, which is more of a problem in soft-water areas where the acidic quality of the water supply leads to gradual corrosion, not only of iron pipework but also of galvanized steel and copper. In soft-water areas, copper hot-water cylinders can suffer from 'pitting' and

'rosette' corrosion, which may cause leaks within ten years. Though other cylinders in the same water area may last twice as long, similar cylinders in hard-water areas may be scrapped after a similar period due to scale formation. One manufacturer quoted a typical average life of a copper cylinder as around fifteen years. Stainless and ceramic-lined steel cylinders have grown in popularity for main's pressure hot-water supplies, as well as for their longer life.

Iron, galvanized and copper pipework may need replacement due to the same furring up or corrosion as suffered in metal tanks. In aggressive conditions, the most practical replacement materials to resist both are now stainless steel, which can provide the closest match to the elegant slenderness of copper where pipework is exposed, and plastics, several of which are marketed for cold, hot water and central heating use, including polybutylene and cross-linked polyethylene. For central heating plastic pipework, it is advisable to use a pipe with an oxygen-diffusion barrier incorporated, which minimizes air infiltration and additive deterioration. Flexible plastic pipe coils allow long joint-free lengths in concealed spaces, so minimizing the possibility of future leaks.

Radiators and Under-floor Heating

The great majority of central heating systems use steel-panel radiators; surviving early examples may well show signs of corrosion, especially at seams and connection points. Later systems have benefited from more effective chemical additives in the primary water, which better protect against corrosion. Once a steel-panel radiator starts to leak, there is no reliable alternative to replacement, although proprietary chemicals can be added to the system to close the leak on a temporary basis.

Cast-iron column radiators seldom show corrosion directly but where they have been re-used, often including a vigorous pre-treatment of paint-stripping, dismantling and reassembly, they are often subject to leaks at the joints. Fan convectors and skirting radiators usually incorporate finned copper pipework and may therefore suffer from corrosion leaks in similar circumstances.

Under-floor heating systems still have a 'leaky reputation' based on the failures of early installations in the 1950s and 1960s, using metal pipework; where the few of these survive, leakage from corrosion or from movement-induced damage may be expected and replacement should be allowed for. However, modern under-floor heating systems using flexible plastic pipework with joint-free circuits have a very good reputation for being leak free. As with any system, there is always some risk of accidental damage, but screeded under-floor heating systems, in particular, are likely to be safest from the carelessly fitted nail or screw.

Workmanship and 'Stress'

There are more common causes of system leaks than corrosion, including poor workmanship in forming joints – it is surprising how many plumbing joints fail at the outset or at an early stage only to seep unnoticed for years because they are hidden out of site and the resulting dampness has caused no diagnosable problem – and sudden stress on joints when water supply or central heating are converted from gravity feed to main's pressure systems. Joints that have performed satisfactorily for many years in a gravity-feed system may spring leaks when subjected to main's pressure; this means that the cost and disruption of converting from gravity-fed to main's pressure systems may be worse than first appears, if all system pipework has to be renewed.

UNDERGROUND LEAKS

Drains

Underground drainage leaks are a frequent source of dampness and often go unnoticed as a cause, simply because they are out of sight. Even a camera survey may not detect leaking drains unless there is an obvious cause, such a cracked pipe or a penetrating tree root.

Drain Testing

If other causes of damp have been ruled out, and the damp is restricted to the vicinity of a drain, the drain run can be tested by closing the pipe with an expandable rubber bung at the downstream end; the bungs can be hired from tool-hire shops. It is always worth placing a brick across the channel in the manhole where the bung has been fitted: this guards against

the water pressure 'popping' the bung and washing it down the next section of drain. The drain is filled up with a hose at an upstream manhole; if the level holds, say for ten minutes, the drain run is free of leaks. If the level drops, it may be possible to locate the level and location of the leak by waiting until the level stabilizes. If the water is half-way down the drain, rather than visible in the manhole, it can be located by feeding a hose down the drain and blowing air down it – when bubbles are heard, it has reached water, and the length of hose can be measured to locate the leak point.

Unfortunately, a drain pressure-test failure does not prove that a drain leaks in normal service, since drains typically 'run' at only a small proportion of their overall capacity, meaning that a crack or partial joint failure in the *top half* of the pipe, which causes failure in the level test, may not actually lead to leakage in normal use. However, repair, lining or replacement may still be appropriate, particularly in the case of root penetration.

Ancient Drains, Culverts and Victorian Improvements
Of course, leak-resistant drains are a relatively recent development in 'modern times'. Historically, drainage was provided by natural streams, ditches and, eventually, culverts, which were usually built of fairly rough stone, often without mortar. More sophisticated culverts had the smoothest stone slabs laid as the bed to improve flow and the rougher slabs used for roofing. Even if mortar was used in joints, it was a lime mortar and the whole drain was generally porous. What culverts lack in watertightness, they often make up for in size, so it is sometimes possible to install a modern drain within a culvert, leaving the culvert to act as a land drain only. It is risky to block up such culverts, even though they may appear disused, since they may work intermittently as land or surface drains.

Although clay drainpipes and asphalt-lined brick drains have been found in Babylon, dating from around 4000BC, and sophisticated drainage systems were developed by the Minoans, Etruscans and Romans, drainage did not begin to develop widely again until the nineteenth century. Hamburg's sewer system was built from 1843 and followed by London's from 1852.

Straight clay pipes had been used butt-jointed since pre-classical times but the mass-produced spigot and socket salt-glazed clayware drainpipe was only developed in the nineteenth century, and then continued in dominant use until the 1960s, except for the extraordinarily successful use of hollow log pipes in the US – in use for over 130 years in some cases – and a parallel growth of pitch-fibre pipes until the advent of PVC and polythene as pipe material. Socketed clay pipes were traditionally jointed with tarred hemp and mortar. Movement causes cracks in the mortar, so many of these joints leak slightly despite working satisfactorily as drains. Seepage from such cracks encourages root invasion, which can worsen the leak and potentially block the drain, so it is sensible to suspect older drains in the vicinity of trees or shrubs.

Modern Drains

Hepworth introduced the first flexibly jointed clay pipes in 1956 and, from the 1960s onwards, clay-pipe drains were increasingly laid in longer and lighter lengths – typically 1.6m (5ft 4in) – with flexible joints, usually of plastic collars with neoprene gaskets. Apart from their improved strength and performance, these drains are as simple to adapt and repair as the plastic alternatives, since sections can be cut out and inserted using chain-type pipe-cutters and the flexible joints slid into place. For small-scale works, alterations and repairs, many builders prefer to use plastic drainpipes and fittings – usually PVC; although lighter to handle, they are no quicker to use and require more imported bedding and backfill material than clay pipes.

Damaged traditional pipes and culverts at substantial depths or below buildings can be lined rather than replaced. There are several proprietary systems for *in situ* pipe lining, which may be worth considering on the basis of a camera survey; though, where it is possible, traditional trenching and replacement will usually be less costly. Although drain camera surveys can be thwarted by interceptor traps and drop manholes, they generally provide a low-cost and comprehensive location and condition survey of drainage, invaluable in assessing leaks and damage.

Concrete pipes are seldom found in houses because they are used for large sizes only, though they may occur close to houses as public storm or foul sewers. At these larger sizes – 300mm (1in) diameter and above – their presence should be marked on water company or local authority drainage maps; the relevant drainage authority will need to be consulted about, and may be responsible for, any repairs needed.

Septic Tanks, Cesspits and Cisterns

These are another potential source of dampness. Septic tanks and cesspits are traditionally built at some distance, and downhill, from a house – 15m (around 50ft) is the current requirement – so leakage from them, which is very common in older masonry and brickwork tanks, is seldom a problem – at least for the house they serve. However, a neighbour's tank or soakaway uphill can contribute to damp problems for houses lower down.

Cisterns are often found close to, or under, buildings where they provided a useful source of water. Unlike wells, which tend to suggest a low water-table, cisterns trap rain or spring water close to the surface and so can effectively raise the water-table.

The first house I bought had seen service as a dye works or laundry in the nineteenth century and had a small stone-vaulted cistern under its garden fed by an underground spring. We discovered it because it lay directly under the foundation line of a new extension we were building. Since this cistern was very much 'live', it seemed best to leave it undisturbed, so we dug foundations both sides of it and carried the new wall on a beam above it. Just as in this case, and of culverts, it is best to leave water courses undisturbed where possible, or if needs be, provide them with a generously sized alternative drainage route, so there is no risk of damming a possible flow and causing dampness or even flooding.

Leak Water Testing

In cases of difficult diagnosis, but where there is liquid water present rather than just dampness, it may be possible to trace it either by tracing dye from a potential source, such as a nearby drain, or by analysis of the water. It is in a water company's interests to find leaks and they should be able to help. A 'leak technician' may be able to locate leaks by listening to the service pipe with a 'listening stick' or with a 'leak noise correlator' – an electronic device that is connected to a pipe each side of the suspected leak and can then indicate the leak location. Gas tests are also used: the section of pipe is drained and filled with hydrogen – leakage of the hydrogen is then detected by a 'sniffer' device.

Leaking main's water becomes ground-water and can travel, so a leak that floods a cellar of house A may originate at house B half a mile away, which makes detection very difficult and perhaps allows us to sympathize with the water company's mammoth task.

Simplification

The virtues of simplicity are worth stressing in this matter of water and drainage services: the more complex a system, the more likely it is to fail and the less likely that its failures will be easily diagnosed and remedied.

So, if the opportunity arises in the course of repairing leaks to sort out and simplify a system, perhaps in a house much altered and adapted over the years in a piecemeal fashion, it is worth taking the opportunity to achieve a simpler and more rational system that is clearly understood by householder and plumber alike. No system is perfect and services especially will need attention for maintenance or alteration, so it is best to keep photographs, notes or diagrams of where the pipework is and where the necessary valves and controls are. It is a simple measure when repair or renewal work is being done to attach labels to valves and to mark pipe runs; a decade later, it may not be so easy to remember which pipe is which.

CHAPTER 6

Remedying the Effects of Damp

After all the analysis of different kinds of dampness in houses, this chapter is more holistic in that dampness, whatever its source, needs similar treatment by way of drying-out and making good. Four useful headings for this area are: time, process, side-effects and finishes.

TIME

Damp-affected houses can be wetter than newly built houses because the porous consistency and sheer bulk of traditional building structures makes modern houses seem spindly in comparison, and because, at least in a new masonry house, despite the eight tons of water typically built into its concrete and blockwork, plaster and paintwork, by the time it is inhabited, much of the water incorporated in its thin structure will have already evaporated and – all being well – no more will have been getting in.

A full-scale refurbishment of an old house does have much in common with a new build. Though the time-scale may be even slower, it usually needs to be, with traditional masonry walls typically 450–600mm-thick (18–24in), there is four to six times as much wet masonry to dry out as there is in the typical 100mm (4in) inner leaf of a modern cavity wall. If a house was built in solid brick, it may be a mere 225mm (9in), or in the case of Georgian houses in Bath, as little as 100 or 150mm (4 or 6in) of limestone.

The cure of problem dampness, whether it is rising or penetrating, should cut off the damp at source but will leave the legacy of damp material.

Drying-Out Rates

The rule of thumb for drying-out of 'an inch (25mm) of masonry or concrete per month' may seem extreme and daunting when faced with an 18in-thick wall but at least a wall has two faces, so as long as it is not sealed in by an impervious cement render externally, or a vinyl wallpaper inside – to take two grim examples – it will dry out in both directions.

Floors are much slower, inch for inch, than walls because they now have DPMs below them that prevent moisture travelling in either direction, so they dry-out upwards only. So, a new 100mm (4in) concrete slab may well take four months to dry and if it is topped by a 50mm (2in) cement-sand screed, it could well take six months – a good reason, amongst others, to omit the screed and finish the slab to a good standard instead. It is therefore not surprising that saturated traditional masonry walls may well take a year to dry after their dampness source has been 'cut off' by the installation of an injected DPC, for example.

For a typical damp-proofing job, householders are unlikely to wait a year before refinishing their interiors, so the remedial work has to allow for the drying-out to continue: it is crucial to the success of such works that both the builders and the householders appreciate how long the whole drying process can take and how to treat the finishes and live in the house so that it can happen painlessly.

THE PROCESS

Flooding

A brief word here about dealing with 'traumatic damp' or flooding, which can range from inundation by your local river to the mere wet floors caused by a burst water-tank or a flooded bath: the two critical factors affecting these drying-out processes will be how long the flood lasted and what material did it bring with it.

The typical internal domestic services 'flood' from a washing machine or overflowing bath is relatively brief and mercifully clean, which makes the cleaning-up and drying-out both quicker and easier. Whereas timber may not have been wet for long enough to get fully saturated, gypsum plaster and plasterboards are so absorptive that they usually show some lasting effects. The key to minimizing the effects is to remove saturated materials, such as carpets, as soon as possible; even if they are simply wet and otherwise undamaged, they will dry out faster and more effectively if taken up and exposed to the air, as will the floor beneath and the surrounding walls and ceiling.

External flooding usually brings with it significant dirt, sludge and sometimes sewage, which makes the remedial work not just drying-out but often scraping-out and cleaning-up, which may necessarily involve more water. Particularly where the floodwater has persisted for some time, there may be serious silt deposits, which may require partial dismantling of floors, ducts, stairs and any framed walls within the flooded zone. Although, in theory – and if the smell was bearable – such deposits could be left *in situ* to dry out, they would be very likely to promote decay and ongoing dampness. Once the flood damage and debris has been thoroughly exposed and cleared away, the remaining dampness can be treated like any other.

Briefly flooded solid masonry walls will be saturated at both sides but may still have a drier core, in which case, drying-out may be quicker than for rising damp or long-term penetrating damp.

Cutting Off the Source

The clear priority is to cut off the incoming damp. Although availability of contractors or obtaining consents may delay the major work, wherever it is possible to safely make short-term repairs, for example to roof coverings or rainwater goods, this should be done at the earliest opportunity, so as to maximize the length of the drying period. The next step is to remove unwanted materials that retain the damp and prevent evaporation, such as ceramic tiles and vinyl

floor or wall finishes. Similarly, wherever claddings, boxings, skirtings and built-in furniture are due for removal, they should be stripped out as soon as possible, rather than left to a later stage.

Drying Conditions

Drying of buildings is much slower than it often appears: surface moisture dries off rapidly but the speed of evaporation of embedded damp is affected by the pore size of the material, temperature and air movement. Fine-pored material is slowest to dry, while evaporation diminishes with falling temperatures and itself contributes to the temperature drop.

As common sense dictates, ideal drying conditions mean heat and rapid ventilation – typified by strong sun and strong wind: natural to the climate of Fuerteventura, perhaps, but seldom to the UK. Since the spring, summer and autumn are the best times for building works, projects are often completed just as winter begins. However, the crucial time when drying-out can happen fastest is much earlier than completion: whether for a new house or a refurbishment, that important milestone in building is when the roof is waterproof. Little wonder then that this is traditionally marked by a 'topping out ceremony': from then on, the building should be getting drier inside rather than wetter.

Flues and Stacks

If there are chimney stacks that will be out of use, it is advisable that vented raincaps (*see* Fig 67) are fitted as early as possible to the chimney pots, so that the flues and stack masonry can begin to dry out. For the same reason, existing fireplaces and chimney breasts – whether or not they are to be retained – should be opened up so as to encourage natural stack effect to aid air circulation in the rooms and to speed the drying process in the flues and stacks themselves.

Windows and Doors

Ideally, there is a period of time before the windows and doors are closed up so that the house has maximum ventilation. If windows are retained in a refurbishment, they should be kept open as much as possible. If windows or glazing are renewed, this should be delayed to allow for that critical airflow. Maintaining this high ventilation rate for as long as possible is important, not just for drying-out the residual moisture in floor slabs and walls, but because the finishing processes themselves introduce more water in plaster and paint.

Fans and Heating

Most parts of most houses have sufficient natural ventilation from doors, windows and flues to dry, if these are kept open, though there may be cupboards, alcoves and under-stair spaces that need some help. Small fans set at slow speed are all that is required to ensure air movement. Fan heaters may be used carefully in extreme cases but there are risks from over-rapid drying, particularly for fresh plaster or unseasoned joinery, which can shrink and crack, so controls should be set at 'warm' rather than 'hot'.

If temperatures are low or weather conditions are poor with frequent rain or mist, artificial heat will be needed and, if it is available, the central heating system should be used while retaining good ventilation. In the presence of new plaster and timber, or of very damp material, it is important that heating systems are controlled so as not to raise temperatures too rapidly. What is needed is just sufficient heat to encourage evaporation from damp surfaces but not so much that plaster and timber shrink and crack.

If winds are strong, it will be more effective to leave windows partially open so that heating effects can be distributed internally rather than blown clean out of the house. Since heating will raise warm moist air towards ceiling level, the most effective place to ventilate is at high level, so the highest available window sashes should be opened.

If the heating system is not available, it is very important that any temporary heating used should not introduce water vapour, as, for example, do flue-less propane-gas heaters and paraffin heaters. In most cases, the simple solution will be electric heating and fan heaters set at a low heat setting will assist with air and heat distribution for even drying.

Dehumidifiers

The same warnings apply to the use of dehumidifiers as to fan heaters: that they should be used in moderation, but preparation for their use needs to be more thorough. The space needs to be sealed at windows, doors, vents and fireplaces from external air and from any source of moisture such as WCs, water-storage tanks and so on – plugs should be fitted and overflows taped over for all sinks, baths and basins, for example – otherwise the dehumidifier may appear to be extracting large quantities of water but may be doing so from the world outside or from your water supply, rather than from the damp fabric of your house. Dehumidifiers with an internal tank need to be checked and emptied regularly; the state of any

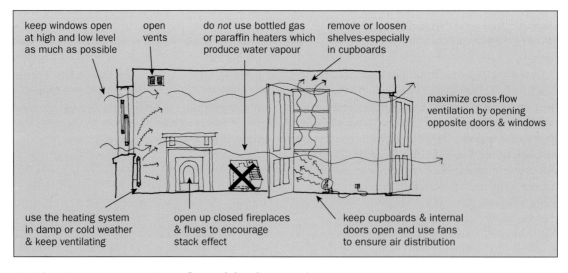

Fig 145   Drying-out: maximize airflow and distribution and raise temperatures.

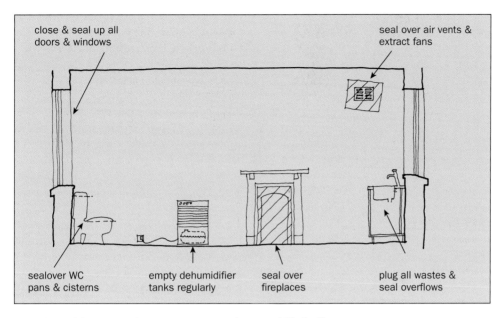

close & seal up all
doors & windows

seal over air vents &
extract fans

sealover WC
pans & cisterns

empty dehumidifier
tanks regularly

seal over
fireplaces

plug all wastes &
seal overflows

Fig 146   Dehumidification: seal rooms against outside air and block all moisture sources.

sensitive material, such as timber or old plaster, should be checked for shrinkage. So, whereas maximizing ventilation for drying is very compatible with refurbishment or building works – many of its processes require good ventilation as a matter of health and safety – dehumidification is not: spaces need to be sealed off for the dehumidifier to do its job effectively.

Damp-Damaged Material

There are two general rules about removal of damp-damaged material.

Plaster on damp walls (as has been discussed in Chapter 2), accumulates salts in the process of the damp evaporating through it. When the source of rising or penetrating damp in a wall is cut off or diminished, by an injected DPC or an external land drain for example, the wall is still damp and that dampness will continue to migrate through the masonry and evaporate from its surfaces for some time to come, perhaps for several months or more. Therefore, the later the salt-laden plaster is removed, the more of that residual dampness and its salts will be taken with it, and the less will remain to migrate into the new plaster. For that process to be effective, the evaporation must be allowed to occur, so any impermeable

finishes, such as wallpapers – particularly vinyl-faced ones – tiling, oil paints and hard cement renders, should be removed at the start, whereas the plaster may be left *in situ* for as long as practicable. If the remedial works are being done in isolation by a damp-proofing specialist, this is unlikely to be workable, since the contractor will need to complete his work within the shortest possible time. On the other hand, if the damp treatment forms part of a wider refurbishment project, it can be worth planning for a delay in the removal of plaster. As mentioned in Chapter 2, removal of historic plasters can risk the loss of wall paintings, so this process may simply be unacceptable. So, if a new DPC is appropriate at all, it may have to be installed without the benefit of the guarantee that is subject to plaster renewal.

In contrast to plaster, decayed timber to be removed should be cleared away as early as possible, since it is likely to inhibit drying of masonry and can serve as a moisture source for fungal attack. Again, with older houses, timber linings may contribute important character and, even if not legally protected, it may be worth considering whether it is worth the extra cost of careful removal, treatment and reinstatement, rather than simply stripping out and disposal.

Removal for Restoration

Very few builders are sympathetic to 'careful removal and reinstatement' of old timber and they will often claim that such material is decayed or too difficult to remove, when what they mean is that it is much more troublesome than the simple alternative of scrapping the old and installing new – for which, ironically, they may then claim additional costs. It may be an appropriate area for the conscientious DIY enthusiast or amateur restorer to expend the necessary time and care to produce a good result.

SIDE-EFFECTS

Shrinkage

The softer building materials, plaster and timber in particular, shrink as they dry out, whereas stone, brickwork and concrete do not do so significantly, and steel and glass do not at all. The lesson worth noting in this respect is just as significant for new building work as for refurbishing damp houses: if finishings and decorations are done too soon, there will be a heavy toll of shrinkage cracking to be rectified six months or a year after 'completion'. For new work, shrinkage from drying-out is exacerbated by setting and seasoning shrinkage but even fully seasoned timbers can expand substantially from dampness.

Dry Rot Conditions

It is important to be aware that 'dry rot' in particular thrives in slightly damp conditions, not in saturated ones. So, as a house dries out from serious damp problems, it will go through a less damp period when it is more liable to dry rot attack. The combination of increasing temperatures and reduced dampness, typical in refurbishment and conversion projects from damp-control measures and new heating installations, is ideal for dry rot.

The degree of dampness that sustains fungal attack in timber is quite specific: a moisture content above 21 per cent. Generally, higher moisture content, nearer 30 per cent, will be needed to set off an attack of dry rot, and much more than this for wet rot. By way of comparison, the typical moisture content for new kiln-dried joinery is around 12 per cent and the majority of structural timbers in roofs, for example,

will retain a moisture content around 15 per cent, varying slightly with the seasons.

Although fungal spores are widespread and therefore the risks of decay likewise, normal living standards, particularly of heating and ventilation, will discourage dry rot – as well as wet rot – and the typical refurbished or damp-treated house will simply pass through a risk period as it dries and warms, and will emerge unscathed.

Locations

The risk areas where drying may be delayed long enough for the rot to take hold and grow are especially those concealed spaces behind pipeboxings, bath panels, skirtings and panelling, and within floor or roof voids close to damp masonry, which can serve a source or reservoir of moisture to feed the fungus. For these reasons too, it is important that the drying process is given access to hidden voids; for example, an exposed masonry wall suffering from penetrating damp and gutter leaks may have had its primary external problems solved by repointing in lime mortar and new rainwater goods, and its interior refinished in lime plaster, but the painted shutter boxes and wainscot panelling below its sash windows may be trapping residual damp and will need to be opened up for inspection at least, and preferably kept open long enough for all that additional moisture in the new lime plaster to have evaporated.

Symptoms

The tell-tale signs of incipient dry rot are the whitish strands or filaments – the mycelium – which can be hard to see initially. Once the timber shows signs of shrinkage and cracking, the rot is more advanced and, if the red dust of spores is found, then fruiting bodies will be present. It is unlikely that a drying-out process will leave time for the spectacular fruiting bodies of the fungus to develop, unless dry rot was well-established already or unless drying is much delayed in confined spaces.

Although dry-rot symptoms may be short-lived, and the fungus die back once the house has dried, it is wiser to investigate at the time, partly to ensure that worse symptoms are not concealed and partly to expose the suspect area to more effective drying and to treatment, if necessary. In contrast, wet rot whitens

Fig 147   Spectacular fruiting bodies of dry rot fungus. (Peter Cox)

timber and reduces it to a stringy substance but the wet rot fungus is unlikely to take hold during the drying of a house.

If in any doubt, advice should be sought from a specialist surveyor or contractor; timber-treatment specialists will usually give initial advice without charge. The conventional chemical solutions to rot are not the only route: Hutton and Rostron [www. handr.co.uk] are probably the best known of the 'environmental school' of treatment specialists and have carried out consistently successful chemical-free treatments of disastrously decayed houses. The process of careful drying and monitoring may take longer than more conventional approaches but can be much less destructive and thereby more economic.

Treatments

In such circumstances, especially where there is time pressure – as there usually is – to refinish and reinhabit the house, it may be worth using a low-toxicity preventative treatment, such as a water-based boron solution, to discourage fungal decay. Although timber to be treated needs to be dried before it can 'take up' the treatment fluid, applying such a treatment will in itself introduce moisture and sufficient time must be allowed for treated timber to dry before it is 'closed up' near to residually damp masonry. Masonry itself may warrant treatment, since dry rot is more than

Fig 148   Advanced dry rot – the white mycelium (to the left) and the fruiting body (to the right). (Peter Cox)

capable of spreading via its filaments across two metres of masonry in search of more timber.

FINISHES

Awareness of the slow pace of drying-out is fundamental to selecting new and replacement finishes.

Damp Tolerance and Permeability

Unless the drying-out can be left to run its full course before finishes are applied, which is seldom feasible, especially if that drying-out is going to take over a year, the new finishes have to be chosen for their vapour permeability and/or their damp tolerance. These attributes have to extend right through the finishes from the original, damp surface. For example, a weak cement–lime–sand render undercoat is both permeable and, to a reasonable degree, damp-tolerant but a finish coat of gypsum plaster, though also permeable, is much less damp-tolerant. Combine these with an oil- or vinyl-based decorative paint, which is neither permeable nor damp-tolerant, and we have a problem in the making. Residual moisture in the wall, instead of evaporating freely, may be trapped by the paint in the gypsum finish plaster, where it will cause swelling, in turn blistering the paint. In some lesser cases, perhaps where external wall surfaces allow good evaporation and the residual moisture can escape that way, the symptoms may not occur.

Rendering after DPCs

As discussed in Chapter 2, specialist contractors installing DPCs in existing walls usually require the replacement of plaster up to at least a metre above the new DPC and supply salt-inhibiting additives for the cement and sand render mix. It is nevertheless important that this render is permeable, so a relatively weak mix, usually around one part cement to five or six parts of sand. It should also be weaker than its background, so if this is built of soft bricks or cob, for example, the mix may be as weak as 1:8 or 1:9.

Although strong cement render mixes may be more waterproof – so tending to mask imperfections in the new DPC – they shrink more and are less tolerant of movement, so cracking is common, which can lead to residual moisture 'escaping' via the cracks and causing local blistering.

Permeable Paints

The problems of trapping residual damp behind ordinary finishes can generally be avoided by decorating in water-based and vinyl-free paints – most 'trade emulsions' and all 'eco paints' are vinyl-free – and substituting lime- or cement-based 'renovating plasters' for gypsum-based plaster.

Inevitable Impermeability

In some situations, impervious finishes may be necessary; for example, ceramic tiles in kitchens or bathrooms, but tiles are very tolerant of damp, provided both their backing surfaces and their adhesives and grouts are moisture-resistant. If these are correct, the wall will have to dry out externally but the tile finish should survive. In some cases, this impervious area may divert and worsen damp symptoms in adjacent areas but, providing the fundamental problems have been dealt with and the damp is residual only, it should gradually dry up.

Timber Panelling

Where timber panelling – or any cladding on timber framing – is to be reinstated or newly fitted to a damp-treated wall, it certainly makes sense to delay fixing the panelling as long as possible, to treat the back face of the complete panelling assembly with a boron preservative, and to allow in the installation for discreet air vents at top and bottom, so that any residual moisture can be vented away rather than being trapped by the panelling.

Sensitive Finish Protection

On rare occasions, it may be necessary to protect a new susceptible finish material, such as wallpaper, from residual damp by tanking the wall. We would generally recommend clients to avoid this by waiting for as long as possible before applying damp-sensitive finishes; if necessary carrying out an initial, simple decorative process, perhaps in white, vinyl-free emulsion.

Finish-Free

An opposite approach is to avoid finishes altogether by exposing the structural surfaces of the house and this will be discussed further in the next chapter.

CHAPTER 7

Living With Damp

Much of the subject matter of this book has been the correction of damp problems and, although some of these problems, particularly those of penetrating damp through damaged roofs or rainwater goods for example, are clearly and fully repairable, there are others, say in the cases of rising damp and interstitial condensation, which may be less straightforward, and some where the 'cure' may seem worse than the malady.

A MODERN PROBLEM

As discussed in Chapter 1, the concept of dampness in houses as a serious problem is a modern one, developing alongside changes in building practice and design that made it feasible to build 'dry buildings' and influenced by a better understanding of public health.

Commercial Interests

As in many other fields, the evolution of damp-proofing houses has also been influenced by commercial interests and marketing. This has certainly been the case with the remedial damp-proofing industry, which has grown substantially on the strength of the electric moisture meter as both diagnostic and marketing tool, backed by the consistency of mortgage lenders and local authorities in demanding 'guaranteed damp-proofing' as a condition of mortgage finance and improvement grants or loans.

Changing Attitudes

There has been some liberalization of attitudes to damp-proofing in the last two decades, influenced both by the success and spread of conservation and environmental philosophies, and perhaps more significantly by the fairly consistent growth in housing values, which has made damp a less significant issue financially. The significant effect of lifestyle on dampness has already been referred to [under Symptoms and Diagnosis in Chapter 1]. As the proportion of damp housing has diminished, so the craft and common sense of 'damp living' has faded into redundancy for most of the population.

Environmental and Conservation Concerns

At the same time, some of the philosophies of the 'eco fringe' have been spreading into the mainstream, particularly within the last few years, as global warming has finally figured in the public and commercial consciousness. In housing design and construction, this has shown most conspicuously in the moves to reduce carbon dioxide generation by reducing energy, especially fossil fuel consumption; but parallel with this trend has been the growing interest in 'greener' construction materials and especially finishes. These trends have developed alongside the growing success and popularity of building conservation, as reflected in its growth as a television subject, and in the recent growth of traditional materials suppliers. These last two issues of 'greener' and more traditional materials are critical to the idea of 'living with damp' in a positive sense.

As referred to in the Introduction, dampness is a natural state for us as human animals: desiccation is bad for us, which is why many of us 'humidify' our centrally heated homes, with indoor plants, aquaria or humidifying accessories to radiators, and why the cosmetics industry does so well out of selling us moisturisers. The principal reason why we need to humidify heated houses to maintain comfort is that we have excluded natural dampness.

While controlled humidification may seem like a better option than abandoning all the successful technology of damp control in modern building construction, it can still seem perverse to expend resources, money and technological ingenuity of only partial effectiveness to damp-proof our existing houses, when more balanced approaches are available to us, often at lower cost.

THE BUILDING FABRIC: SYMPTOMS AS PROBLEMS

Problems for Solutions

All leaking services and the majority of penetrating-damp symptoms are undeniable problems: whether the puddle of water is due to a roof leak or a damaged pipe, the repair needs to be made and, mercifully, these are the easier problems to solve.

Solutions by Alternative Approaches

However, the tide-marks, peeling paint and erupting plaster of rising damp in walls are usually a reflection of the ways the wall has been treated, an indication of the unsuitability of internal finishes more than a serious moisture problem as such.

The quantity of moisture producing these symptoms in a vinyl-emulsion painted, gypsum-plastered, solid masonry wall is not dissimilar to the quantity we offer to our potted plants from the watering can. If we re-run the same scenario with the masonry walls, lime pointed and unfinished, we have avoided paint and plaster costs and have a 'breathing wall' that can comfortably release rising damp without ill effects. If the quality of the masonry is not up to public display, the wall can be lime-washed or lime or earth plastered without adversely affecting its permeability.

Serious rising damp in traditional walls and floors will carry salts and deposit them at the surface where evaporation occurs. Where this salts problem is severe, probably including hygroscopic salts that attract

Fig 149   The peeling paint and erupting plaster of rising and penetrating damp.

atmospheric dampness, even when the water-table is low, there may be no alternative but to strip and refinish the wall, which at least creates the opportunity to decide whether finishes are necessary at all: traditional masonry or brickwork, well cleaned and lime mortar pointed, can be very attractive in colour and texture, and can be dust sealed with vapour-permeable clear or pigmented finishes, if necessary.

A Balanced Approach to Dampness

In comprehensive refurbishment, the balanced approach to dampness lowers a high water-table with land drains just above foundation level and does not overload the walls with rising damp by installing new DPMs in the floors but includes solid floors laid over free-draining gravel or lightweight expanded clay aggregate (LECA) – like clay versions of maltesers without the chocolate – for better insulation and continuing vapour permeability.

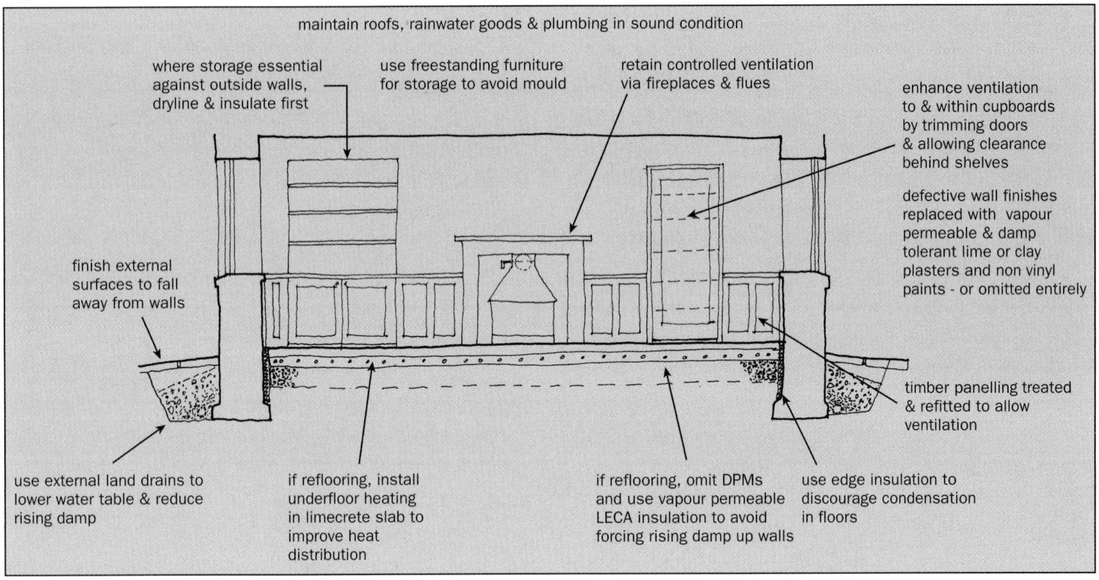
maintain roofs, rainwater goods & plumbing in sound condition
where storage essential against outside walls, dryline & insulate first
use freestanding furniture for storage to avoid mould
retain controlled ventilation via fireplaces & flues
enhance ventilation to & within cupboards by trimming doors & allowing clearance behind shelves
defective wall finishes replaced with vapour permeable & damp tolerant lime or clay plasters and non vinyl paints - or omitted entirely
finish external surfaces to fall away from walls
timber panelling treated & refitted to allow ventilation
use external land drains to lower water table & reduce rising damp
if reflooring, install underfloor heating in limecrete slab to improve heat distribution
if reflooring, omit DPMs and use vapour permeable LECA insulation to avoid forcing rising damp up walls
use edge insulation to discourage condensation in floors

Fig 150 Living with damp.

Severe Cases Needing Diversionary Tanking

There are locations and damp pressures so severe that a balanced permeable approach will not be enough. In which case, diversionary tanking of the platon type – the 'chocolate box lining' material – is the consistent partner detail, allowing for free drainage and/or air movement.

LAYOUTS AND LIFESTYLES

These measures relate to the fabric of the house but there are many other aspects of sensibly living with damp that relate to layouts and lifestyles.

Heating and Ventilation

Accepting and living successfully with damp in traditional buildings involves an effective balance of heating and ventilation. The traditional approach of focussed radiant heating by air-guzzling coal fires with large flues is not morally viable in our carbon dioxide burdened biosphere; but low-temperature, well-distributed radiant heating – typically underfloor – is an ideal partner to a still damp house, as well as being most adaptable to non-fossil fuel heat sources. Good distribution is the key to its success as damp management, both in mitigating the symptoms of rising and penetrating damp, and in minimizing the risks of condensation by raising all internal surface temperatures.

Out of the heating season, ventilation becomes the over-riding issue. Whereas principal rooms are usually well enough ventilated by their windows, doors, flues and vents, and the activities of living in them, the troublesome areas tend to be windowless storage rooms and cupboards, especially if they are fully occupied. The simple measures of ventilating cupboard doors by trimming them short at base and head or perforating them with holes can have only a limited effect if the whole cupboard is stacked solid with 'goods'.

Storage Management

Significant improvements can be made by using slatted shelving – as for airing cupboards – or by simply drilling air holes through the backs of cupboard shelves. For utilitarian storage, flexible systems of shelving bracketed to vertical metal rails (or timber battens) have the added advantage of setting the shelves away from the wall, which allows air to circulate behind. Storage arrangements that make use of baskets or boxes to contain the goods stacked on shelves have a better chance of maintaining some air circulation.

Cupboards and stores against outside walls tend to perform worst, since they are more prone to penetrating damp and condensation. If there is no alternative to this type of location, it may be necessary to dryline and insulate these particular outside walls, which will reduce the risk of local condensation and damp.

Historically, our forebears had the great advantage of possessing far fewer goods for which to find storage space, and the canny habit of using free-standing pieces of furniture on legs – chests, cupboards, drawers and wardrobes – well clear of the floor, to isolate their stuff from the damp houses they inhabited. Clearly, 'fitted kitchens' and 'built-in wardrobes' are the opposite to this and tend to maximize closed spaces, often against cold and damp external walls.

The normal arrangement of bedrooms on upper floors, as well as increasing security, provided clear advantages in keeping clothes, beds and bedlinen well above the level of rising damp.

Finally

Finally, beyond the floods, leaks and condensation and their remedies, the householder's attitude to dampness can be a matter of personal choice – for those of us who have that luxury. For those who enjoy living in traditional houses in their traditional, damp state, the symptoms of dampness are just another aspect of life, a little like the weather but fortunately more within our control.

Some aspects of that control are in simple choices and routines that avoid or mitigate the more troublesome symptoms of damp. Others are in matters of finishing materials and methods that may require a little more care and thought to achieve but need no significant extra investment of capital or labour. Yet others are in more substantial physical measures of renewal or improvement that may – but do not necessarily – include the most sophisticated technologies of modern damp-proofing.

Damp problems often seem grim at first sight but diagnosis and available solutions can work wonders. The purpose of this book has been to equip readers with an overview of the many options available, so as to be able to assess many problems for themselves and, where further expert advice is needed, to give them the basic understanding and confidence to judge what they are told and to select the appropriate remedies.

FURTHER READING

Brunskill, R.W. *Illustrated Handbook of Vernacular Architecture* (Faber and Faber, 1971)
Melville, Ian A. and Gordon, Ian A. *The Repair and Maintenance of Houses* (Estates Gazette, 1973)
Powys, A.R. *Repair of Ancient Buildings* (SPAB, 1995)
Thomas, A.R., Williams, G. and Ashurst N. *The Control of Damp in Old Buildings* (SPAB, Technical Pamphlet, 1992)
Trotman, P., Sanders, C. and Harrison, H. *Understanding Dampness* (BRE Press, 2004)

BRE Digests (DG) and Good Repair Guides(GR):

GR5 *Diagnosing the Causes of Dampness* (Jan. 1997)

GR6 *Treating Rising Damp in Houses* (Feb. 1997)

GR7 *Treating Condensation in Houses* (Mar. 1997)

GR8 *Treating Rain Penetration in Houses* (Apr. 1997)

GR23 *Treating Dampness in Basements* (Mar. 1999)

GR30 *Remedying Condensation in Domestic Pitched Tiled Roofs* (May 2001)

GR33/1 *Assessing Moisture in Building Materials Part 1: Sources of Moisture* (Sep. 2002)

GR33/2 *Part 2: Measuring Moisture Content* (Oct. 2002)

GR33/3 *Part 3: Interpreting Moisture Data* (Nov. 2002)

DG163 *Drying-out Buildings* (Mar. 1974)

DG180 *Condensation in Roofs* (1986)

DG245 *Rising Damp in Walls: Diagnosis and Treatment* (1986)

DG297 *Surface Condensation and Mould Growth in Traditionally Built Dwellings* (1990)

DG369 *Interstitial Condensation and Fabric Degradation* (Feb. 1992)

DG380 *Damp-Proof Courses* (Mar. 1993)

GLOSSARY

Batts, insulation Semi-rigid slabs of insulation material suitable for building into construction cavities between masonry, timber and so on.

Breathing construction Designed and built to allow the controlled passage of air and water vapour.

Cavity 'bridges' Debris, etc., in a cavity that potentially allows moisture to cross from outer to inner wall.

Cavity tray Pitched DPC across a cavity used to divert moisture to the outer wall.

Cavity wall Three-element construction that uses a cavity between inner and outer walls to resist the passage of moisture.

Chase Groove cut in masonry to accommodate flashing (etc.).

Clay lump Unfired clay cut into blocks or 'lumps' for construction.

Cob *In situ* wall construction of mud built up in shallow layers without shuttering.

Cold roof Insulation at ceiling level leaves roof structure and finish cold and liable to condensation without vapour check and roof-space ventilation.

Condensation Moisture arising from water vapour meeting a cold surface.

Construction moisture Water incorporated in building works from wet construction trades, such as concreting, masonry, plastering and decorating.

Copings Weather-resistant top details to walls.

Counter-battens Battens fixed over sarking along lines of rafters to support battens clear of sarking for drainage and ventilation.

DPC Damp-proof course: waterproof layer in wall construction.

DPM Damp-proof membrane: waterproof layer in floor construction.

Drylining Boarded internal finish, usually on battens or adhesive dabs.

Electro-osmotic DPC Suppression of capilliary action in a wall by inducing charge in the material.

Fines Fine aggregate in concrete or mortar.

Flashings Typically in roofing; flexible, waterproof, strip material used to link one material or surface to another, so as to exclude moisture.

Flaunching Mortar finish to falls around chimney pots on stack.

Floating floor Unfixed floor boarding – usually tongue and groove with glued or clipped joints – laid over a vapour check and insulation layer.

Gradient of permeability Arrangement of construction layers to ensure that the most permeable are towards the outside and the least permeable towards the inside.

Hairline cracking Cracking of less width than (human) hair.

Heads, window/door Lintels/beams over wall openings.

Hip (roof) Angled, external corner junction between adjacent roof slopes.

Interstitial (condensation) Occurring between the layers of construction.

Jambs Vertical edge element of framed joinery, e.g. side of door or window.

Land drain Perforated drainpipe laid below ground to collect/dispose of ground water.

Masonry Stone, brick or blockwork construction.

Mortar droppings Scraps of mortar dropped accidentally by builder in cavity that can accumulate at ties or base of wall to form 'bridges'.

Mortar fillets Triangular section application of mortar to join adjacent surfaces, typically roofs to adjacent walls, chimneys and so on.

Newtonite lath Vertically corrugated pitch-fibre sheeting designed to isolate plaster from damp walls, leaving an air space behind.

Nibs Projections on underside of tiles that allow them to be hooked over battens.

Parging (also torching) Application of *in situ* material (lime mortar, clay, hair, straw, etc.) to underside of tiled/slated roof to reduce draughts and rain/snow penetration.

Passive stack Extract ventilation without mechanical power; works through stack effect.

Penetrating damp Rain or snow penetrating under wind pressure or gravity.

Perpend Vertical joint between adjacent bricks, stones and so on.

Platon membrane Three-dimensional semi-rigid plastic diversionary tanking that avoids water-pressure build-up by retaining cavity.

Pointing Mortar fill to external joints of masonry.

Rainscreen cladding Ventilated cladding relies on sarking behind for effective weatherproofing.

Rainwater goods Guttering and rainwater downpipes.

Rammed earth Walling of semi-dry subsoil rammed between shutters.

Reveals Sides of an opening in a wall, e.g. the depth of wall to each side of a window.

Rising damp Ground moisture drawn up porous construction by capilliary action.

Rodding Clearance of blockages from drain pipes by use of drain rods.

Salts Mineral crystals left behind in walls or floors by evaporating moisture, can be hygroscopic – attracting atmospheric moisture.

Sarking Water-resistant layer below tiling to provide back- up weather-resistance.

Screeding Sub-finish to solid floors, usually of sand and cement/lime, used to level and smooth a rough sub-floor or slab, prior to the application of internal finishes.

Sheathing Boarding over rafters below counter-battens/battens for structural/weather-proofing/insulation retaining reasons.

Tanking The waterproof lining of buildings to keep moisture out.

Thermal mass Dense construction material, e.g. masonry, concrete and so on, that serves to stabilize internal temperatures by absorbing/re-releasing intermittent heat gains.

Trickle vent Minimal passive ventilator typically incorporated over windows.

Underpinning Structural support of walls by building below them – usually in short sections.

Upside-down roof Insulation outside roof membrane, deck and structure; avoids condensation risk without ventilation and protects membrane.

Valley (roof) Angled internal corner junction between adjacent roof slopes.

Vapour barrier Fully sealed layer in construction prevents the passage of water vapour.

Vapour check Layer in construction generally resistant to the passage of water vapour.

Wall ties Structural links or straps between inner and outer walls of cavity construction.

Warm roof Insulation above roof structure; avoids condensation risk without ventilation.

Water-table The natural level of moisture in the ground – varies seasonally.

Weepholes Open perpends to allow drainage of wall cavities at cavity trays.

INDEX